Bushido and Christianity

Bushido and Christianity

Sasamori Takemi

Translated by
Mark Hague

Published by Reigakudo Press

2016 Takemi Sasamori

The author has asserted his right to be identified as the author of this book. All rights reserved. No part of this publication may be reproduced, stored in a retrieval system, or transmitted, in any form or by any means, electronic, mechanical, photocopying, recording or otherwise, without the prior permission of the author.

First published in Japanese in Tokyo, Japan in 2013 by Shinchosa Inc.

First published in English in Tokyo, Japan in 2016 by Reigakudo Press

ISBN-10: 1533476675
ISBN-13: 978-1533476678

Printed by CreateSpace

Front cover photo by Kojin. Cover layout and design by Kai Lee Hague

Available from Amazon.com and other online stores

Contents

TRANSLATOR'S ACKNOWLEDGEMENTS VII

FOREWORD IX

CHAPTER 1: THE MISSION OF WARRIORS IS TO STOP CONFLICT 1

CHAPTER 2: THAT WHICH COMES AFTER COURAGE AND PERSONAL SACRIFICE 22

CHAPTER 3: SEARCHING FOR AN INVINCIBLE SCHOOL OF KENJUTSU 34

CHAPTER 4: HEARTS FILLED WITH BOTH BUSHIDO AND CHRISTIANITY 60

CHAPTER 5: LOOKS CAN BE DECEIVING 72

CHAPTER 6: DOES CHRISTIANITY ACCEPT RITUAL SUICIDE; IS THERE LOVE IN BUSHIDO? 98

CHAPTER 7: EXAMINING THE CONCEPT OF 'ME' THAT IS NOT FOUND IN BUSHIDO 122

AFTERWORD 146

WORKS CITED 149

APPENDIX A: ONO-HA ITTO-RYU LINEAGE CHART (ABBREVIATED) 150

Conventions

Japanese terms have been romanized according to the Hepburn system and italicized on their first appearance. Long vowels are denoted by macrons. Common Japanese terms and phrases that appear in the *New Oxford American Dictionary* are written without italics or macrons. Japanese and Chinese personal names are written in the order of surname followed by given name.

Principal Periods of Japanese History	
Nara	710-794
Heian	794-1185
Kamakura	1185-1333
Ashikaga (Muromachi)	1336-1573
Warring States (Sengoku)	1467-1568
Azuchi-Momoyama	1568-1600
Tokugawa (Edo)	1603-1867
Meiji	1868-1912

Translator's Acknowledgements

Figure 1: Sasamori Takemi, 17th Soke of Ono-ha Ittō-ryū, and Mark Hague, translator.

It was a great honor to be asked by the author to translate his life's work and personal philosophy into English. In the pages of this book, the Rev. Sasamori describes how discussing both Christianity and Bushido can help people, and I count myself as a beneficiary. While translating the book, I suffered the loss of a close family member and found both solace and inspiration in the words of the author.

I would like to thank the Rev. Sasamori for his support, guidance, and seemingly limitless patience as I navigated the nuances of topics that eluded me in both languages. With his encouragement, I added annotations where I thought the non-specialist in Japan would find it useful. I would also like to thank Karen Johnson for her review of the initial draft, Nathan Scott and Mamie Lee for their insightful comments, Chris Loew for his tremendous support in editing, and Kato Tomoko and Nathan Frost for their assistance in translation.

While those mentioned above provided essential help in the translation process, any and all mistakes are mine and mine alone.

Map of Japan

Foreword

I work as a minister at Komaba Eden Church, a Protestant church my father created in our house in Tokyo. This church is in Daizawa, Setagaya Ward, an area of the city where no church had ever existed, and it has been spreading the word of God for over forty years. Every Sunday over one hundred people come to worship.

As mid-sized churches go, it is nothing special, but there is one difference between it and others: after worship services end the chairs are put away and it converts into a martial arts training hall, or *dojo*, where about thirty students practice Japanese swordsmanship, or *kenjutsu*.

Their teacher is me, once I change out of my business suit and into a practice uniform. I am not only a kenjutsu instructor, but also serve as the seventeenth *sōke*, or headmaster, of an ancient school of fencing that has existed from the Sengoku period called Ono-ha Ittō-ryū. Ittō-ryū is a style of kenjutsu created by the sword master Ittō Ittōsai and contains the secret prescription, "No matter what, go forward and strike down your opponent with one cut." It is no exaggeration to call it a formidable method of swordsmanship. During the Edo era, kenjutsu masters from Ittō-ryū, along with expert swordsmen from Yagyū Shinkage-ryū, were selected to be official instructors to the Tokugawa shogunate. It is also considered to be the root of modern kendo.

Tsukue Ryunosuke, the protagonist of the novel, *Daibosatsu toge* (大菩薩峠),[1] written by Osaragi Jiro (大佛次

---

[1] The novel *Daibosatsu toge* was made into a movie of the same name in Japan, but titled *Sword of Doom* when produced for foreign audiences. Trans.

郎), likely knew Ittō-ryū because he used a special stance that is also found in Kogen Ittō-ryū. Kogen Ittō-ryū is a fencing school that split away from Ittō-ryū at the time of the second-generation sōke. The niece of Osaragi Jiro was related to my father's private secretary, and she and her friends often came to our house to gather source material for his novels.

It seems that I am the only one in all of Japan who could be called a kenjutsu sōke who simultaneously serves as a Christian minister. Every year I take trips to Europe and America to teach Ono-ha Ittō-ryū, but no matter where I go, I have yet to hear of another person who shares these same roles. In the chapters ahead, I will give my personal history in detail, and when I explain how I came to be both a sōke of kenjutsu and an ordained minister it may surprise those associated with Christianity and the martial arts alike.

I am constantly asked if there is an inherent contradiction between the two. Every time someone poses this question, I reply, "No, not at all. If you are interested, why don't you come to our church and see for yourself? I think you will find it is the only church like it in the world." I suppose I generate interest among many people because I avoid answering their questions directly.

About twenty years ago, I was consulted by the Keisen School for Young Women, a Christian school in Tokyo. Faculty members were discussing the creation of a kendo club and were debating whether it was appropriate for students to practice Japanese martial arts in the school. I was invited to visit and took the opportunity to explain that there are no inconsistencies between the Japanese martial arts and Christianity since there are aspects within both that are surprisingly alike. As a result of this discussion, the administration decided to establish a kendo club. After that, people from other Christian schools approached me for similar consultations.

Some people associated with Christianity think that Bushido should not co-exist with Christianity and that the two are incompatible because they are from different worlds. They regard Bushido as barbaric, since it gave birth to various forms of martial arts that were designed to kill, as opposed to Christianity, which advocates peace and love. Perhaps the Christian church continues to oppose Bushido as a means to preserve its own power while Bushido continues to fade away.

Certainly, there are big disparities between Bushido, which describes moral precepts and proper behavior, and Christianity, which is a religion. But they are both Ways that examine how people live and die. They both address life and death, and consider a life that presumes death. In other words, they look at life based on how one dies and deeply contemplate death based on how one lives.

I would like to give an example. It is commonly believed that Bushido was established during the Edo era, but a much older spiritual foundation exists. A book that illustrates this is the *Tōsenkyō* (闘戦経), written around 1100. The author, Oeno Masafusa, was a Confucian scholar of the late Heian period. This book begins with the passage:

> In the beginning, our martial virtue (*bu* 武)[2] existed in the universe, and then, in an instant, cleaved

---

[2] This character normally appears in compounds and is rarely used alone. Nelson provides the following contemporary definitions for the character appearing by itself: military affairs, military arts, chivalry, military glory, military power, arms, and

apart Heaven and Earth. This was like a chick pecking through its egg... Consequently, our martial virtue is the wellspring of all things and the origin of hundreds of schools.

To clarify, martial virtue existed in the cosmos from the beginning of time and in a mighty blow separated Heaven from Earth. This is just like how a baby bird is born into the world when it pecks its way out of the shell of the egg that surrounds it. Accordingly, the Way that leads to martial virtue turns into the wellspring, source, or energy that creates everything. You will probably figure this out right away, but the contents of this book are not so much aimed at teaching the ABCs of martial arts but are more metaphysical and philosophical in nature.

The wide magnitude of the words, "In the beginning," probably brings to mind in many the famous quote from the Bible, "In the beginning was the Word, and the Word was with God, and the Word was God." (John 1:1 Revised Standard Version [RSV]). The term *Word* has its roots in the Greek word *logos* and has various meanings, such as *theory*, *truth*, *ideology* and *learning*. When translated into Meiji-era Japanese it was rendered as *michi* (道), meaning "Way." This word refers to such things as how people live their lives, the ideal state of society, universal laws, truth, and the source, as well as the power to put these ideals into practice, and I try to explain to people that the phrase in the Bible, "In the beginning was the Word," is just like what is written in the *Tōsenkyō*.

---

bravery. Andrew N. Nelson, *The Modern Reader's Japanese-English Character Dictionary*, Second Revised Edition [Vermont: Charles E. Tuttle, 1962]. Trans.

Those who know Bushido well have probably heard of highly educated men like Nitobe Inazō and Uchimura Kanzō who emphasized the commonalities between Bushido and Christianity. Uchimura left behind correspondence he exchanged with Christian missionaries in which he discussed death as it relates to Bushido. It seems that some of these missionaries criticized Bushido as not being compatible with Christianity because it advocated ritual suicide and revenge. Uchimura always defended Bushido, arguing, "There are many of the Christian faith who seem to believe that Christianity is the enemy of Bushido. However, I don't agree with this."

In fact, Uchimura and Nitobe were not the only Japanese who encountered Christianity and had the good fortune of embracing both it and Bushido within their own homes. A great number of missionaries and ministers traveled to Japan at the beginning of the Meiji era, and descendants of samurai families and former members of the warrior class, including Uchimura, approached them and enthusiastically accepted the Christian faith, which had been prohibited in Japan for over 260 years.

Nitobe, who continued to pursue Christianity while a student in America, later published the book, *Bushido: the Soul of Japan*. The book was well received in the United States and became famous for the deep impression it made on President Teddy Roosevelt. It was also translated into the languages of many Christian countries in Europe. Why did this book become a best-seller? I believe it is because Christians were able to identify with the material inside.

Even today, you can see a similar phenomenon. Japan has an unusually strong relationship with America, an advanced Christian nation. Why does a nation that once fire-bombed Japan and that possesses nuclear weapons continue to be regarded as the most-liked country by the Japanese in public opinion polls? What brings about the very close, top-level relationships between our leaders, such as those between Prime Minister Nakasone and President Reagan or Prime Minister Koizumi and President Bush? Why are the movies of film director Kurosawa Akira, such as *The Seven Samurai* and *Yojimbo*, which show the sacrifice and emotional side of the Japanese, being remade in Hollywood? I just heard talk that *Chushingura* is in production as the *Forty-Seven Rōnin*. In my observation, Japan's bonds with non-Christian countries are not nearly as strong. Could it be that this mutual interest between the Japanese and people from Christian countries is because they share the same sense of values with those who outwardly appear to be different? If so, why?

Unfortunately, Japan is considered a barren wasteland to evangelical Christians. Few Japanese have embraced Christianity, and the total number of Christians in Japan has reached less than one percent of the population. Since I was young, I have often questioned why the Christian faith was not more prevalent throughout my country. Perhaps one reason is that it came to Japan too late in our history. Another may be that it was transmitted to Japan from Western nations and tended to be thought of as a "Western" religion. However, Christianity originated in the Middle East, not in Europe. If Christianity had come to Japan through Asia rather than Europe and had been accepted within Japan a long time ago, I wonder if it would have spread more widely. This is certainly my personal view, but I have no doubt that the Japanese people have deep connections to both Bushido and Christianity.

In this book, I will look back at the history of Christianity in Japan in the post-Meiji era and then examine in detail where Christianity and Bushido intersect. Perhaps the commonalities and touch-points between the two will enlighten readers who have never before considered them. I think the reader will come to view Japanese history and culture from a different perspective. At the same time, I would also like to explain, in an easily understood way, some key lessons of Christianity, such as how we should learn to accept ourselves as we are and the concept of the soul, neither of which are addressed by the code of Bushido.

I believe this new perspective may offer a ray of hope in the midst of a society in which chaos and confusion will only deepen. This is not merely theory. Through discussions I have had with many people who have visited Komaba Eden Church burdened with life's troubles, I have seen that discussing both Bushido and Christianity can help.

To begin, I will start with a discussion of Nitobe Inazō and Uchimura Kanzō, both of whom managed to live through the turbulent Meiji Restoration.

Note: I quote scriptures from the Bible throughout this book. The section of the Bible from which they are quoted is cited as in this example, (John 1:1 RSV). Many people know this, but the Bible is divided into two books, the Old Testament, which covers the time before Christ, and the New Testament. Some people may think that the Gospels are separate and distinct from the Bible, but this is incorrect. They have always been essential books of the Bible. For example, "The Gospel According to John" is considered to be a record of Jesus' sermons written by John, who was one of the twelve disciples. When you see the phrase, "The Gospel According to __" or "The Record of __," please insert the name of the person who was thought to have written the Gospel in the empty space. However, from recent research, we are learning that the Gospels could have been written and compiled by students of those who were thought to have been the original authors.

Chapter 1

The Mission of Warriors Is to Stop Conflict

The Warriors Who Were Born Too Late

"When Yamato Takeru swung the 'Grass Cutting Sword' that came from the tail of Yamata no Orochi, the dragon slain by Susanoo no Mikoto, he produced a shower of sparks that allowed him to escape from danger…" Since the mythical age, when this legend appeared in the *Kojiki*,[3] the sword has been considered a treasured item in Japan. It is well known to be one of Japan's Three Imperial Regalia.[4]

Kenjutsu, which means how to fight with a sword, blossomed during the Muromachi period. Later, during the Sengoku period, the number of schools teaching kenjutsu multiplied, and it was in this era that the sword master Ittō Ittōsai Kagehisa created Ittō-ryū, in which I serve as the sōke.

Then, when did Bushido appear? If you look at the works written at the beginning of the Edo period (1603-1867) by the Confucian scholar and strategist Yamaga Soko, he used the words *budo* (武道)[5] and *Shido* (士道).[6] Also, in

---

[3] The *Kojiki*, translated as, *The Record of Ancient Matters*, is the oldest chronicle of ancient Japan and dates to the eighth century. It is also considered a sacred text of the Shinto religion. Trans.
[4] The other two treasures are a mirror and a jewel. Together they represent the three virtues of valor, wisdom and benevolence. Trans.
[5] Literally, *the way of the warrior*, but more commonly translated

the middle of the Edo period, around 1716, Yamamoto Tsunetomo, a retainer of the Saga Domain, recorded his understanding of proper samurai conduct in a book titled *Hagakure*, in which the term *Bushido* (武士道) first appeared. So, the term *Bushido* first started to be used around this time.

Yamamoto was born nearly half a century after the siege of Osaka Castle, in an era when peace prevailed throughout Japan, and the samurai of that time were far removed from the realities of the battlefield. However, they were never without their swords, and if asked if they would die for their lord, had to reply that they would. Moreover, even though they were a privileged class that presided over the affairs of commoners and were prohibited from engaging in farming or commerce, they were compelled by necessity to re-examine their metaphysical raison d'être and what it meant to be a warrior or a gentlemen all the more.

It was for this reason that Bushido, which was originally derived from military tactics and martial skills employed on the battlefield, came to be regarded by the samurai of that period as an important way of life. You could say that Yamamoto, who focused on the ethical behavior of the samurai in his book *Hagakure* and was a great admirer of past historical eras, was born too late.

The values of Bushido, as articulated by Yamamoto, were widely shared among the warrior class of that time. Seen from a Western perspective, this probably stands out as odd because, unlike in Christianity in which there are written scriptures in the Bible that dictate moral behavior, the code of Bushido was never written down anywhere.

---

as *martial arts*. Trans.

[6] Literally, *the way of the gentleman*. Trans.

The ethical values of Bushido, including what was considered manly and what was considered devious, spread to even the lowest members of society through cultural traditions like Kabuki and Bunraku, literature, and word of mouth. I think that we should consider the Bushido of today to be the merging of practical martial skills used on the battlefield with this existential view of life that was prevalent during the Edo period. Though the requirement to serve one's lord had not changed, the essence of this activity changed from warriors fighting their enemies on the battlefield to battling against themselves through daily training in martial arts.

What Is the Essence of Bushido?

In short, what is Bushido? I consider it to be showing compassion toward an opponent. They say that martial arts begin with proper conduct and end with proper conduct, and that people who practice any of the wide variety of martial arts in existence study techniques so that they can defeat anyone. The fact is, however, that Japanese martial arts have never been a Way that called for killing people.

The Japanese character *bu* (武), which forms the first part of the word *Bushido*, when broken down into its component characters, refers to stopping a spear. Since the earliest recorded history of Japan, *bu* has been interpreted to mean stopping or preventing conflict. Special dictionaries of ancient Chinese glyphs note that Chinese characters written on tortoise shells show that the ideogram now recognized as meaning *stop* (止) originally meant *footprint*, so the character *bu*, which contains ideograms for both a footprint and a spear, was interpreted at the time to mean to advance while holding a weapon, or to engage in combat. However, in the Chinese literary classic *Spring and Autumn Annals,* written during China's Warring States period, the following appears: "*Bu* means to stop the spear. Thus, as ruling monarchs, they said the way to preserve their kingdoms was to put away spears and arms, put their bows and arrows back in their quivers without using them, and act with virtue." (The King of Chu cited this from a poem extolling the Zhou dynasty written by King Wu of the Zhou.)[7]

Even if the character *bu*, in its original permutation in ancient China, meant *to fight,* by the end of Japan's Jomon period the definition had changed to mean *keeping the peace*. Japan adopted its writing system from China around this time, so this character has been defined as deterring or stopping violence from before the beginning of Japan's recorded history. Even the *Tōsenkyō*, the Heian period book on martial arts, records that "Soldiers exist to ensure the peace and tranquility of society." The purpose of *bu* was to rid the world of suffering. More simply, the purpose of *bu* was to prevent civil strife and maintain tranquility throughout the land. It is for this reason that people learn the sword, bow, *naginata*, jujitsu and other martial arts.

In fact, Ittō-ryū is taught along these guidelines. To grow food, you first must cultivate a field with a hoe. To cultivate a field, you have to hold a hoe and swing it into the dirt. This movement corresponds to the single cut of a sword. Making a cut with a sword is not done to destroy but to cultivate a person's mind and create a better society. <u>Therefore, the process of training</u> with a sword should be

---

[7] Confucius. *The Spring and Autumn Annals.* N.p. [thought to have been written 722-481 BCE and edited by Confucius some time later.]

done to improve one's character. Incidentally, in the English language, the root of the word *cultivate* is *culture*.

Bushido has never been a Way to make yourself stronger so you can do things like dominate others. It is about making a conscientious effort to foster a safe environment and create a world where people are respected and have compassion for each other.

Aside from kenjutsu, the warriors of the Edo period also studied the Zhu Xi School of Neo-Confucianism. This school was created by Zhu Xi, a scholar who lived in China during the Song Dynasty, and it was introduced to Japan during the Kamakura period. It was later adopted as the orthodox philosophy of the Tokugawa Bakufu thanks to the efforts of the Edo-period Confucian scholar Hayashi Razan. Characterized by the central theory of "knowledge first, then action" (知先行後), it was favored by the ruling elite in both China and Japan as a means to maintain law and order.

However, as the end of the Bakufu drew near, the number of samurai who subscribed to the Wang Yangming School of Confucianism started to increase. This school, created by Wang Yangming (1472-1529), a scholar during China's Ming Dynasty, emphasized the importance of taking action, as summarized by the saying, "knowing, but not doing, is the same as not knowing" (知行合一). Nakae Tojū, a philosopher of the early Edo period, was a famous proponent of this doctrine.

The samurai who subscribed to the Wang Yangming School criticized the traditional political structure in which authority was centralized around the shogunate. These warriors thought that matters should be decided through debate after first gathering and considering a wide variety of opinions. History shows that the central figures in the

Meiji Restoration, such as Yoshida Shōin, Takasugi Shinsaku, Saigō Takamori, Kawai Tsuginosuke, and Sakuma Shōzan, were students of the Wang Yangming School, and later they even contributed, albeit indirectly, to the spread of Christianity among the warrior class.

The Prayers that Converted the Spies

Every schoolchild in Japan learns about the period of our history when, in 1612, Tokugawa Hidetata issued a decree banning Christianity for 260 years, and a small group of Christians, known as *Hidden Christians*, continued to practice their faith in secret. However, most do not learn how Christianity spread throughout Japan before the government lifted this ban in 1873. The descendants of samurai families played a prominent role in that effort.

While many feudal domains were still adjusting to the social upheaval that accompanied Japan's entry into the Meiji era, the rulers of these domains sent their most talented young men to Kyushu and Yokohama. Before the feudal system was abolished and prefectures established in 1871, these leaders still had a great deal of autonomy and tried to get their young men to study English and Western education from the newly arrived missionaries and other foreigners. However, this was not their only motivation. They also assigned their young charges the duty of covertly finding out what these missionaries were up to and reporting back to them.

One of these missionaries active in Yokohama at the time was James H. Ballagh. Arriving in Japan before the ban on Christianity had been lifted, he could not openly display his Christian beliefs, so he taught English and medicine to Japanese students while biding his time until he could practice his faith in public. He had up to sixteen pupils in his school, which he called the *Ballagh Juku*, and he used the Bible as his textbook when he taught English. Some of his students were spies sent from various feudal domains or Buddhist temples. Their daily interaction with Ballagh, however, brought about a religious transformation.

In lieu of formal churches, the missionaries in Yokohama started to conduct prayer meetings that allowed them to continue to worship in private. At first, those who were sent to spy secretly listened in on the sermons, thinking, *I wonder what these missionaries are up to? Are they putting some kind of curse on Japan?* However, in the course of their eavesdropping they heard some shocking messages, such as: "The citizens of Japan are very good people. It is okay to sacrifice us, but please be sure to save them." The Japanese had been persecuting Christians for decades and the missionaries understood this all too well. Nevertheless, they still fervently prayed for the salvation of the Japanese people. This had a profound impact on the spies sent to Ballagh's school and made them all the more curious about what these missionaries really believed.

There is an episode that provides a glimpse into the resolve of these missionaries. At the time, many Japanese were hostile toward Christianity, and there was the real possibility that some harm could come to foreigners when they ventured out of their residences for a walk. While some of his contemporaries hired bodyguards for their protection, Ballagh refused, saying, "I believe that in Japan, a nation which values Bushido, there are no cowards who would attack an unarmed foreigner." This made the Japanese who heard this feel that he truly understood the genuine spirit of Japanese Bushido.

One of the young men who studied at the Ballagh Juku was Nimura Morizō. Nimura was sent to spy on Ballagh's school by the Grand Council of State (*dajōkan* 太政官),[8] but he converted to Christianity and ended up devoting his life to establishing the Church of Christ in Japan (*Nihon Christo Kōkai* 日本基督公会), Japan's first Protestant church. Through their experiences in Yokohama, many of the warriors of Japan's samurai class came to hold in high esteem the missionaries, who not only risked their lives taking a long voyage to Japan but were even willing to become martyrs for the sake of their beliefs.

In March 1872, the Church of Christ in Japan was formed with Ballagh working as a provisional minister. When the ban on Christianity was lifted a year later, his young charges began studying the Bible in the open, and some even decided to become baptized. Among those studying under Ballagh in Yokohama, nine students received their baptism, and two of them joined the Church of Christ in Japan.

This church produced such notables as Uemura Masahisa, from a family of former vassals to the Shogun; Oshikawa Masayoshi, a retainer from the former Matsuyama Domain; and Ibuka Kajinosuke, a retainer from the former Aizu Domain, all of whom were later active in spreading Christianity. Due to the close connection they had with each other and other like-minded Christians they pulled into their circle, they formed what became called a "band," and their particular group came to be known as the Yokohama Band.

---

[8] This was the precursor to the modern Cabinet system. Trans.

The Young Samurai Who Wanted to Be Baptized

As in Yokohama, groups of young men from samurai families also gathered in bands in far-flung Kumamoto and Sapporo, and these three bands became the wellspring of Protestantism that spread throughout Japan in the post-Edo period. Among those who belonged to the Sapporo Band were Nitobe Inazō and Uchimura Kanzō. Before delving into their personal histories, I would like to describe the Kumamoto Band.

The Kumamoto Domain, which accepted the rule of the Emperor rather late in the Meiji Restoration, wanted to provide their young men from samurai families an education in Western studies, so in 1871 they invited Captain Leroy L. Janes, an active-duty officer from the United States Army, to Kumamoto to open a school. His school came to be known as the Kumamoto Yōgakkō. Janes even taught the Bible in his home and, by 1875, was engulfed in a storm of religious fervor from his students. The next year, thirty-five of them gathered on Mount Hanaoka, near Kumamoto Castle, and swore an oath, "The Christian Prospectus" (*Hōkyō Shuisho* 奉教趣意書), vowing to save their homeland through Christianity.

Some of the more famous members of this group were Ebina Danjō of the former Yanagawa Domain (later president of Doshisha University); Kanamori Michimoto, a retainer of the former Kumamoto Domain (later a minister); Yokoi Tokio of the former Kumamoto Domain (eldest son of Confucian scholar Yokoi Shōnan and later president of Doshisha University); Ukita Kazutami of the former Kumamoto Domain (later a doctor of law and head of the teaching department at Waseda University); and Tokutomi Iichirō (later Sōhō) a retainer of the former Kumamoto Domain. Unlike those in the Yokohama Band, where many people were lifelong evangelists, those in the Kumamoto Band seemed to show more interest in social issues than religion, building futures in academia, politics, and the business world.

The activities of the young samurai invited resistance from the more conservative elements of Kumamoto, and after only five years the Kumamoto Yōgakkō was forced to close its doors. The students then appealed for support from Niijima Jō, who founded Doshisha University after returning from the United States, and consolidated their school with his in Kyoto.

The Sapporo Band was formed after the Kumamoto Band and was composed of young college students who converted to Christianity while studying at Sapporo Agricultural College (currently Hokkaido University). The college opened in 1876 for the purpose of educating those pioneers who settled in Hokkaido in administering the reclamation and development of land. The Director General of the Land Development Bureau at the time, Kuroda Kiyotaka of the former Satsuma Domain, established the college. While visiting the United States to conduct preliminary research prior to opening the school, Kuroda singled out William Smith Clark, better known in Japan as Dr. Clark, to assist him.

Clark, then serving as President of the Massachusetts Agricultural College, accepted Kuroda's requests for help but did not resign before setting out for Hokkaido. He took a one-year sabbatical instead to assist Kuroda. During the era of ocean travel it took many weeks to make a round trip between Japan and America, so Clark could only spend eight months of his year in Japan. However, despite being given the title of vice principal and only spending a short time at the school, he played an active part in every aspect of the college.

It is well known that there was a short period of discord between Kuroda and Clark. Though Kuroda left the ethical education of the students up to his vice principal, Clark structured his lessons around religious tenets contained in the Bible. Kuroda strongly objected, asserting that "In Japan we have Shinto and Confucianism. Why must you use the lessons of Christianity to teach ethics?" Kuroda was acutely aware that the Kumamoto Yōgakkō was closed down in 1876 and was concerned his school would suffer the same fate. But Clark's positive attitude and pressure from the students who attended his lectures won over Kuroda, and Clark received formal permission to teach the Bible to his students.

In reality, Clark did not view himself as a missionary or a minister when he served as vice principal; he saw himself as nothing more than a devoted acolyte. He was a Puritan. The Puritans were a faction of Protestants that separated from the Church of England in the sixteenth century and are famous for crossing the Atlantic and landing in North America where they were the driving force behind the establishment of the United States. Every morning, before class, Clark would hand out English language Bibles and lead his students in Bible study, prayers, and hymns. His lectures were based on lessons from the Bible that emphasized that the mere pursuit of material wealth was meaningless, and that one should live a life based on spiritual values and faith.

An Additional Parting Gift from Dr. Clark

As he had planned from the beginning, Clark departed Sapporo in April 1877. He is famous in Japan for his departing words of, "Boys, be ambitious!" but he actually left an additional going-away present. The month prior to his departure he created an oath, "The Covenant of Believers in Jesus." This oath stated:

> The undersigned member of Sapporo Agricultural College, desiring to confess Christ according to his command, and to perform with true fidelity every Christian duty in order to show our love and gratitude to that blessed Savior who has made atonement for our sins by his death on the cross; and earnestly wishing to advance his Kingdom among men for the promotion of his glory and the salvation of those for whom he died, do solemnly covenant with God and with each other from this time forth to be his faithful disciples, and to live in strict compliance with the letter and the spirit of his teachings...[9]

All sixteen of the inaugural class of the college signed this covenant. To reiterate, the purpose of the Sapporo Agricultural College was to produce technically skilled experts who would later run Hokkaido under the auspices of the Hokkaido Land Development Bureau. It did not have the mandate of producing clergy, nor was it even a Christian school. This all came about because Dr. Clark's

---

[9] Clark, William. Prepared for the students of the Sapporo Agricultural College. "Covenant of Believers in Jesus." Sapporo: 1877.

personality and outlook on life greatly influenced his students in much the same way that Ballagh transformed those who went to Yokohama to spy on the missionaries at his school.

Those who signed the covenant included Kuroiwa Yomonoshin, a former retainer from Tosa (son of Kuroiwa Ruiko, and later a specialist in animal husbandry); Itō Kazutaka, who hailed from a merchant family in Edo (later the first manager of the Fishery Department of the Hokkaido Prefectural Government); Satō Shōsuke, a former samurai from the Nanbu Domain (later the first president of Hokkaido Imperial University); and Ōshima Masutake, who hailed from a prestigious family from the former Sagami Domain (later a Christian minister and educator).

Of those first year students who signed the covenant, aside from one who had already been baptized, all received baptism from Merriman Harris, a Methodist missionary who had been active in Hakodate.

The Surprise Attacks on Nitobe and Uchimura

Eighteen students matriculated into the second class of the Sapporo Agricultural College after Clark returned home to the United States. Among them were Nitobe Inazō and Uchimura Kanzō. Nitobe had a natural curiosity about new things, while Uchimura was more conservative, holding fast to the traditions of Japan. These two, together with Miyabe Kingo (later to become a professor and botanist at the Sapporo Agricultural College), attended the Tokyo National English School and became very close friends. This school started as the English Department of the Tokyo Foreign Languages School, but split off and later merged with the Tokyo School of Foreign Studies Preparatory School, becoming the First Higher School under the Imperial education system. When they entered the Sapporo Agricultural College, Miyabe was eighteen years old, Uchimura was seventeen, and Nitobe was the youngest of the three at sixteen.

Figure 2: Nitobe Inazō

Nitobe was born in 1862 in Morioka as the third son of Nitobe Jūjirō, a samurai of the Nanbu Domain. (Nitobe had two older brothers and four younger sisters.) This domain fought on the losing side of the Ōuetsu Reppan Alliance, so Nitobe was the child of a so-called defeated samurai family. His father died when he was five, and his mother thought it best for him to be adopted by his uncle, Ota Tokitoshi, so he could pursue his studies in Tokyo where Tokitoshi ran a tailor shop. Nitobe took the name Ota but later changed back to Nitobe in 1889 after the death of his oldest brother (by that time his second oldest brother had died as well). His name changed many times throughout his life, but I will refer to him as *Nitobe* throughout this book. By studying at the Tokyo Foreign

Languages School, Nitobe's path to the University of Tokyo (renamed the Imperial University after 1886) lay ahead of him. However, the newly established Sapporo Agricultural College very generously offered to exempt students from tuition and provide food, lodging, uniforms, textbooks, and school supplies, all free of charge, and also pay students for working at school. This was too hard for Nitobe to resist.

Born in 1861 as the eldest son of Uchimura Yoshiyuki, a samurai of the Takasaki Domain, Uchimura Kanzō had a similar upbringing. (Uchimura came from a family of six boys and one girl.) As a youth, he attended an English language school within Takasaki, but at the age of twelve travelled to Tokyo to study at a private English language school, then transferred to the Tokyo Foreign Languages School a year later. Like Nitobe, he experienced the economic hardship that came with being the son of a so-called defeated samurai.

Dr. Clark had since departed the campus of the Sapporo Agricultural College, but the students at the school still embraced Christianity with a passion. Nitobe was the first to be enthralled by the spiritual education of Christianity and converted in less than a year.

Uchimura described what his first year was like at the school:

> I was then a Freshman in a new Government College (Sapporo Agricultural College), where, by an effort of a New England Christian scientist (William Clark), the whole of the upper class (there were but two classes then in the whole college) had already been converted to Christianity. The imperious attitude of the Sophomores toward the

> "baby Freshmen" is the same the world over, and when to it was added a new religious enthusiasm and spirit of propagandism, their impressions upon the poor "Freshies" can easily be imagined. They tried to convert the Freshies by storm; but there was one among the latter who thought himself capable of not only withstanding the combined assault of the "Sophomoric rushes," (in this case, religion-rush, not cane-rush), -but even of reconverting them to their old faith. But alas! mighty men around me were falling and surrendering to the enemy.[10]

Uchimura eventually submitted to their pressure.

> The public opinion of the college was too strong against me, which it was beyond my power to withstand. They *forced me* to sign the covenant somewhat in the manner of extreme temperance men prevailing upon an incorrigible drunkard to sign a temperance pledge. I finally yielded and signed the covenant. I have often asked myself whether or not I should have held out and not given in to the coercion. I was but a mere lad of sixteen then, and the boys who thus forced me "to come in" were all much bigger than I. So you see, my first step on the road to Christianity was a forced one, against my will, and (I must confess) even a little bit against my conscience. The covenant I signed was as follows....[11]

---

[10] Uchimura, Kanzo, *How I became a Christian: out of my diary*, Tokyo: Iwanami Bunko, 1895
[11] *Ibid.*

The covenant he signed was none other than the 'The Covenant of Believers in Jesus' that I described earlier.

Faith works in mysterious ways. It was only natural for Uchimura to become a Christian after first being pressured into it, but he later became more devoted than anyone and ended up as the de-facto representative of the Christian community in Japan. In fact, he cheerfully recalled that, before he converted to Christianity, he worshiped at Shinto shrines on a regular basis but saw no need to continue this practice after he found the one true God.

Among the eighteen students of the second class of the Sapporo Agricultural College, fifteen signed the covenant. In June of 1878, seven of those who signed received their baptism by Merriman Harris, the missionary from Hakodate. Before long, Nitobe, Uchimura, and Miyabe formed their own assembly, which they called a *small church* (independent church). They adopted the Christian names of Paul, Jonathan, and Francis, respectively, and diligently practiced their faith. The following episode illustrates this.

Mourning Their Friend's Loss

In July 1880, after his fourth year in school and after having been away from Morioka for eight years, eighteen year-old Nitobe set out to visit his hometown. After he departed, however, a telegram arrived at his college informing him that his mother was gravely ill. Not imagining in his wildest dreams that she would be dead, he arrived at his home just in time to meet her remains. He flung himself over her casket in tears and then collapsed on the ground with grief.

A letter arrived from Uchimura Kanzō, who had heard the sad news. Nitobe opened it, thinking there was no way anyone could understand what he was feeling, and read that seven of his closest friends, to include Uchimura and Miyabe, were doing such things as fasting and praying, united in imagining what kind of suffering it would be like to lose their own mothers. They sent along the following passage from the Bible: "Rejoice with those who rejoice, weep with those who weep."[12] This lifted his spirits and helped him begin to overcome the depth of his sadness.

Uchimura and his companions also likely referenced the "Sermon on the Mount" in which it is said that Christ gathered his disciples around him on a mountain top. This sermon is represented by the passages: "Blessed are those who mourn, for they shall be comforted… Blessed are the meek, for they shall inherit the earth… Blessed are the merciful, for they shall obtain mercy."[13] Taking such an extreme measure as fasting as a way to mourn the death of a friend's mother is one of the ways in which Uchimura and his samurai compatriots put into practice the lessons of the Bible.

Why did young men from samurai families from Yokohama, to Kumamoto, to Sapporo find Christianity so appealing? I would offer two reasons. The first is that many of the foreign missionaries and ministers they came into contact with were military men who had served in the Union army during the American Civil War. Janes, who established the Kumamoto Yōgakkō, had been an active-duty lieutenant. Dr. William Clark started the war as a major and resigned his commission as a colonel, and Merriman Harris, the missionary who baptized both

---

[12] Romans, 12:15 RSV
[13] The Gospel According to Mathew, Chapter 5 RSV

Nitobe and Uchimura, had also served in the United States Army. What they all had in common with their samurai charges was the disciplined lifestyle of the warrior. It is not incomprehensible to think that the young men of Japan, flushed with recent memories of the Boshin War and Meiji Restoration, found the values contained in the code of Bushido to be the common bond between them and these veterans of the American Civil War.

The second reason relates to the Wang Yangming School of Confucianism that I touched upon earlier. Uchimura pointed out the similarities between this school of philosophy and Christianity:

> So, unlike the conservative Zhu Xi School (of Confucianism) fostered by the old government for its own preservation, the Wang Yangming School was progressive, prospective, and full of promise. This similarity to Christianity has been recognized more than once and it was practically interdicted in this country on that and other accounts. 'This resembles the Wang Yangming School of Confucianism. Disintegration of the empire will begin with this.' So exclaimed Takasugi Shinsaku, the famous Chōshū strategist and samurai of Revolutionary fame, when he first examined the Christian Bible in Nagasaki.[14]

Ebina Danjo, a Christian of the same generation as Uchimura and who would later become the president of Doshisha University, stressed that he accepted Christianity

---

[14] Uchimura Kanzo, *Representative Men of Japan: Essays*, Tokyo: 1908

precisely because he studied the Wang Yangming School of Confucianism.

> I (Ebina) broke through the barrier and looked toward Christianity because I embraced the practical learning (of the Wang Yangming School). The Zhu Xi School taught that if you admonished your parents three times and they did not listen, you could do nothing but obey them through your tears, however, because the Wang Yangming School dealt with the world on the basis of one's conscience, it provided a road to advancement for the sake of the world even if one defied their parents.[15]

It was natural then that the samurai who followed the Wang Yangming School, which advocated combining reality with the ideal and stressed the importance of following one's personal convictions, would be drawn toward Christianity.

I will describe in some detail later that Jesus Christ followed a similar approach in the Holy Land as he set about saving people's souls and liberating their minds with single-minded devotion. The Roman prefects who represented the power and authority of the Roman Empire, the clans of Sadducees who administered local laws, and other officials who enforced these laws, however, considered him to be a troublemaker who disturbed the peace and threatened to overthrow the existing political order. They arrested him and then had him crucified on the cross to secure their own political power.

---

[15] Watase Tsuneyoshi, *Ebina Danjo sensei*

After Uchimura and Nitobe graduated from college, what direction did their lives take? How did they further develop and incorporate both the Christian faith and Bushido into their daily lives? In the next chapter, I would like to address these questions by letting them explain in their own words.

Chapter 2

That Which Comes After Courage and Personal Sacrifice

How Was Morality Taught in Japan?

I would like to begin by first discussing Nitobe Inazō. After graduating from Sapporo Agricultural College, he took up a post at the Hokkaido Land Development Bureau as stipulated under the terms of his scholarship. After that, he transferred to Tokyo Imperial University but felt something was missing and used his own money to travel to the United States for foreign studies. There, he attended meetings of Quakers, a Christian denomination, and converted to that religion. He met his wife, Mary Elkinton, through the Quakers.

Though the Quakers are part of the Christian world, they are a third major denomination, differing from both Protestants and Catholics, and are known for having strict views on faith. They are unwavering pacifists. The Quakers also build up various powers of insight through what they call the *Inner Light*.

The word *Quaker* comes from the fact that devout believers begin to rock back and forth while they enter into a deep meditative state. While in this state, they believe they can hear God's words and gain spiritual insight. Therefore, when worshiping, they do not need a pastor or minister to perform sermons but sit in quiet meditation.

Their numbers are few worldwide, but there are Quakers in England, Africa, and the United States.

After Nitobe returned to Japan, he became an educator, holding positions as a professor at Kyoto's Imperial University, principal of the First Higher School under the former Imperial education system, and the founding president of Tokyo Women's Christian University. In 1920, he was posted as an under-secretary general of the League of Nations, but his most unforgettable accomplishment was his book *Bushido: the Soul of Japan*, which he published in English in 1899 to introduce the Japanese way of thinking to the world.

Nitobe's motivation for writing *Bushido* is described in the preface of his book. In short, about ten years before writing it, a professor in Belgium posed the question: "If there is no religious education in Japan, how do you impart moral values to Japan's youth?" Not being able to reply led him, with the help of his wife Mary, to trace the values that underpinned both Japanese philosophy and culture.

When he examined this question, he realized that the Bushido that existed in Japan served as the model for the moral precepts of that country. Once he made the association between Bushido and morality, he compiled his observations in book form and then set out to inform the West about Japanese Bushido.

Japan had just won the Sino-Japanese War when his book was published and *Bushido* aroused great international interest in Japan, not just from the United States, but from the rest of the world as well. The book was translated into many languages, including German, French, Polish, Norwegian, and Hungarian.

What did Nitobe, a man baptized as a Christian at the young age of sixteen, think of Bushido? In what way did he believe it was connected to Christianity? After studying much research material and reviewing his own description of it in his book, *Bushido*, I have drawn the following conclusions.

When Nitobe introduced Bushido, he explained that it included five moral precepts: rectitude or justice, courage, benevolence, politeness, and veracity. He also included honor, loyalty, and self-control as important elements. Rectitude comes first because it is the most fundamental of the moral values to a samurai. Simply stated, this refers to people doing what is right.

Nitobe then noted that courage, or valor, if not done in the pursuit of justice, has no meaning and such things as love and magnanimity, which have been considered the highest of virtues since ancient times, lose all value if they lack justice. Nitobe added benevolence next after courage and valor when he listed the five main traits of Bushido.

With regard to benevolence, Nitobe wrote, "We were warned against engaging in indiscriminate charity, without seasoning it with rectitude and justice."[16] Nitobe pointed out that the code of Bushido calls for mercy to be shown toward the weak, downtrodden, or vanquished, and that this same code says to crush arrogance and build a path to peace.

Bushido, in the eyes of Nitobe, was a path to pursue justice as one who is thirsty pursues water or one who is hungry pursues sustenance. Those who followed Bushido, such as the samurai, did not put a premium on written religious scriptures but held action, more than anything

---

[16] Nitobe Inazō, *Bushido: the Soul of Japan*, 1969.

else, as the highest ideal. Because of this, Nitobe believed that Bushido was the best path for people to follow.

> Christianity in its American or English form--with more of Anglo-Saxon freaks and fancies than grace and purity of its Founder—is a poor scion to graft on Bushido stock. Should the propagator of the new faith uproot the entire stock, root, and branches, and plant the seeds of the Gospel on the ravaged soil (in Japan)? Such a heroic process may be possible... [but] is a process which Jesus Himself would never have adopted in founding His kingdom on earth.[17]

Nitobe held Bushido in high regard, but pessimistically foresaw a future in which Bushido would disappear along with the demise of the warrior class. But the first Japanologist from America, William Griffis (later a minister), who was featured in the preface of the tenth edition of *Bushido*, was more optimistic.

After working as an educator in Fukui, Griffis remarked that, even though the samurai as a social class was disappearing, Bushido continued to exist in the hearts of the Japanese people and was the source of their spiritual vitality. He developed this firm conviction after observing first-hand how cultured and polite the people whom he came into contact with were. While quoting the "Metaphor of the Grain of Wheat" in which Jesus said, "except a grain of wheat falls to the earth and dies, it remains alone; but if it dies, it bears much fruit," he wrote that the spirit of Bushido will survive as the wisdom carried forth by the

---

[17] *Ibid.*

Japanese people. I will discuss this later in more detail but feel compelled to point out his keen insight here.

We Need neither Churches nor Ministers

Uchimura Kanzō was also a prolific writer on Bushido and Christianity. Like Nitobe, after Uchimura graduated from Sapporo Agricultural College, he took up a post at the Hokkaido Land Development Bureau and later paid his own way to the United States to study. After he returned to Japan, he worked as a minister and news correspondent, and published many books. In 1900, he published Japan's first magazine about the Bible, *Seisho no kenkyū*, which became his lifework that he continued to publish until his death.

Uchimura is known for creating the Non-Church Movement. This refers to independent worship, the most defining characteristic of which is that it rejects organized churches. Uchimura asserted that, because churches did not exist during the time of Jesus Christ, neither ministers nor clergy are required today. Instead, those known as Qualified People within this movement deliver sermons to gatherings of the faithful, but in the final analysis, all people need to do is read the Bible and abide by its lessons.

The Catholic Church has a much more hierarchical organization than the Protestant denominations, with the Pope and Archbishops at the top, exercising authority over the Vatican. Uchimura thoroughly rejected this hierarchy, noting that the Bible never contemplated such an organizational structure. He argued that it was not necessary to hold the sacraments of communion and baptism under the authority of any church. The only thing that was important was one's faith in Jesus Christ.

Instead of organizing churches, Uchimura and those he gathered around him threw themselves into studying the Bible. As an example of their dedication, the Qualified People who gave lectures were so dedicated that not only did they read the New Testament of the Bible in English and Japanese, but also learned to read it in Greek and Hebrew as well. Uchimura first coined the term *Non-Church Movement* in his first book, *Kiristo shinto no nagusame*, in which he outlined his opposition to the traditional approach to faith. He made this announcement after he had returned to Japan from foreign studies at a seminary in America.

In fact, some say that Uchimara became disillusioned with Christianity during his time studying there. He attended the Hartford Theological Seminary in Hartford, Connecticut. This seminary has a long history in the United States and influenced the development of the theological seminaries at Harvard and Yale universities. I feel that I may have some insight into why Uchimura adopted the Non-church Movement.

As you will read in chapter five, I also attended the Hartford Theological Seminary. I still remember like it was yesterday an encounter I had with a professor when I first started my studies there. He said, "We have autographs here from Japanese people" as he showed me into one of the offices. When I entered, I indeed saw Uchimura's autograph and notes with signatures from various presidents of Japanese universities they had kept. As I perused the material, the professor said, "We educated them." The way he said it, which implied, "We, from a developed nation, taught the uncultured nations," left a deep impression on me. I went there in the 1950s – many generations after Uchimura attended. This professor was merely looking down his nose at me but using more contemporary language, and I imagined it must have been the same for Uchimura and his colleagues.

Perhaps in Uchimura's heart of hearts, this treatment made him start to doubt and reject organized churches in which priests officiated. Or perhaps the seeds of doubt were planted while he was a student at Sapporo Agricultural College and he, Nitobe, and others established the Independent Church that was not affiliated with any denomination.

Though Uchimura rejected everything about organized churches, this does not imply that he rejected the teachings of Christianity. To the contrary, it is clear that he suffered as a Christian while diligently putting into practice the lessons of the Bible. Certainly, there must have been times when he agonized over this. Later, when his daughter Rutsuko was eighteen and near death, we know that he allowed her to be baptized in a Protestant church so she could go with God.

Grafting Christianity onto Bushido

It is clear from reading Uchimura's literary works that his views on Bushido and Christianity are more defined than Nitobe's. Uchimura described his own beliefs as *Christianity grafted onto Bushido*. It is noteworthy that both Uchimura and Nitobe used the keyword *graft*. *To graft* refers to the technology of artificially cultivating plants and agricultural crops by cutting off a branch or scarring the trunk of plant *A* that is growing and attaching to it the branch of plant *B*. Once attached, the branch of plant *B* survives by living off of plant *A*, and this can increase plant *B*'s harvest and resistance to disease. A famous example is how apples are grown by grafting, resulting in branches that do not grow too big and trees that are easier to harvest.

It is critically important when grafting plant *B* onto plant *A* that both are compatible with each other. The fact that both Nitobe and Uchimura used the example of grafting when describing the relationship between Bushido and Christianity shows they were both led to the same conclusion that these two Ways had much in common and that melding them together would give rise to a new value system. Uchimura, in particular, highly valued the ethics of Bushido, writing:

> Most issues of our lives will be dealt with through Bushido. Be honest, be honorable, be magnanimous, keep your promises, do not go into debt, do not pursue an enemy who is retreating, do not take pleasure in the misfortune of others; these are things that we do not need Christianity for. We will deal with these issues through the code of Bushido that has been passed down from our ancestors.[18]

However, he also considered Bushido to be incomplete, so he emphasized the importance of Christianity.

> Regarding our duty to God, our future judgment, and the path to both of these, Bushido teaches us nothing. We have no choice but to turn to the religion of Christianity when confronted with important questions such as these. Those who are Christian are not beneath the Japanese samurai.

---

[18] Uchimura Kanzo, *Shinko chosaku zenshu*, Tokyo: Iwanami Shoten, Volume 23

> Those who cast aside Bushido or look down on it cannot be expected to be good followers of Christ. Those who God seeks from among the Japanese people, especially, are those who allow Christianity to dwell in the spirit of the samurai.[19]

The ethics that are part of the Christian faith were already being practiced within Bushido and would have been familiar to any Japanese person. It was because religious salvation was not an element of Bushido that Christianity was still necessary. Religious salvation is about how you should view yourself as you live your life and what is to become of you after you die. I will discuss why it is important to address these two questions in more detail later in this book.

Uchimura asserted that it was really the Christian who embraced Bushido who was the image that God sought in the Japanese people he himself created. Why was it only Bushido that was incomplete? Uchimura explained that no matter how lofty the ethics of Bushido, in the final analysis, it was a philosophy created by man, so it could not be perfect. Something that was perfect could come only from God. It is only logical that, when Christianity becomes fused with Bushido, the power of God added to Bushido will lead to a perfectly complete belief system.

God, who is the Creator of all things, shows his existence in all things he creates. Westerners believe that Christianity is something bestowed upon man by God. Uchimura pointed out that the Japanese people, as well, are God's creation, so it is only natural that the existence of God be evident in the Japanese. Bushido is the evidence of his existence.

---

[19] *Ibid.*

> Those who are created by God are children of God... we Japanese prove his existence in us, which is only a fraction of his light. It is my belief that Bushido is the greatest of blessings that God has bestowed upon the Japanese people.[20]

Which Country Has the Most Pious People?

But Uchimura did not stop there. He further explained that Christianity without Bushido was morally deficient. This was clear by observing how nations that identified themselves as Christian started wars and other conflicts and by how they treated the weak. He noted that, even in Japan, the behavior of those who considered themselves Christian did not live up to the standards of the samurai.

Bushido was needed, even by Christians. The proof was that it was the samurai who made the finest Christians. Below is an easy-to-understand explanation of Uchimura's theory of grafting.

> Christianity grafted upon Bushido will be the world's finest product. It will save not only Japan but the whole world. Now that Christianity is dying in Europe, and America, due to its materialism, cannot revive it, God is calling upon Japan to contribute its best to his service. There was a meaning in the history of Japan. For twenty centuries God has been perfecting Bushido with this very moment in view. Christianity grafted onto Bushido will yet save the world.[21]

---

[20] *Ibid.*

Both Uchimura and Nitobe viewed Christianity and Bushido through similar ethical lenses. But when Uchimura took into consideration the samurai attitude toward courage and the spirit of self-sacrifice, he concluded that Christianity was the better choice:

> Bushido places great value on courage and self-sacrifice, but when you consider Christ on the cross, the way of life pointed to by Christianity is far superior. Therefore, it was due to this spirit that many warriors came to embrace Christianity at the end of the Meiji era. Once they discarded their prejudice against it and saw it for what it was, it was only natural that they became devoted servants of Jesus.[22]

To what degree did Uchimura and Nitobe, who both advocated the spread of Bushido throughout the world, actually practice martial arts? This is a good question. Perhaps they liked the martial arts but did not practice any. Of course, coming from a samurai lineage, they would have been familiar with Bushido, however, this does not mean they diligently practiced the martial arts every day. I think that one of the reasons Christianity was not more widely accepted in Japan is because those who made the martial arts a lifelong pursuit did not incorporate Christian philosophy into their daily practice. Perhaps if Uchimura and Nitobe had taught the martial arts, they may have been able broaden the appeal of Christianity within their own country.

---

[21] *Ibid.*
[22] *Ibid.*

Wishing that Nitobe and Uchimura had been talented martial artists may be unfair. As educators and scholars, they left behind many great accomplishments, and this is because they came into contact with Christianity, were baptized, and received a proper education while they were still in high school.

I certainly have not accomplished the remarkable deeds of these two but share a similar history in that I was born into a samurai family that once served the Tsugaru Domain and, like them, came in contact with Christianity at a young age. This is the reason I am a minister who doubles as the Sōke of Ittō-ryū. In the next section I will talk about the personal approach both my father and I have taken as sōke when it comes to teaching Ittō-ryū. I will also introduce key points and lessons of this school.

Chapter 3

Searching for an Invincible School of Kenjutsu

What Is the Secret Technique of Kiriotoshi?

The climax of a samurai movie—two warriors, swords drawn, glare at each other across a grassy plain. Step-by-step, they inch closer, searching for weaknesses in each other's defenses. Finally they strike, their swords clashing together. They both freeze, back-to-back. The next moment, one falls dead…

Simply put, this is the secret aim of Ittō-ryū. This is also called *kiriotoshi* (切落). In the technique of kiriotoshi, you move forward and topple your opponent with a single cut of your sword. It also teaches you how to maneuver your body and manipulate your sword to survive a fight, even if both sides cut at the same time.

Even in situations where your opponent is not finished with one cut, the point is still to beat him using kiriotoshi once you block his blows with various defensive techniques. A sword blade will not hold its edge for very long when cutting into flesh due to fat and viscera in the human body. Therefore, all schools of kenjutsu, without exception, looked for ways to eliminate superfluous techniques from their repertoire. However, the defining characteristic of Ono-ha Ittō-ryū, in which I serve as the sōke, is that our school stresses, perhaps more than others, the concept of defeating an opponent with a single cut.

Ittō-ryū literally means the "School of the One Sword." The term *One Sword* (*ittō* 一刀)[23] comes from the sword master Ittō Ittōsai who founded this tradition during the Sengoku period after realizing the universal principle: "All techniques begin with One Sword, and all return to the One Sword." Hence, he named his style of swordsmanship Ittō-ryū and changed his own name to Ittōsai (一刀斎).

So, what is Ono-ha Ittō-ryū, and why has it been transmitted from generation to generation for four hundred years? How does it differ from other kenjutsu traditions, and what are typical training sessions like? In this day and age, what kind of person wants to learn an ancient style of sword fighting? In this chapter, I will begin by introducing the ABC's of Ittō-ryū.

First, I would like to clarify the terms *kenjutsu* and *kendo*. The term *kendo* existed in the Edo period, but the more commonly used term at the time was *kenjutsu*. At the start of the Bakumatsu period, kenjutsu matches in which the bamboo sword (*shinai* 竹刀) was used became popular, and these contests came to be called *gekken* (撃剣) to differentiate them from kenjutsu. This naming convention continued into the latter half of the Meiji era when the term *kendo* took hold. This naming convention was likely influenced by Kano Jigoro, the Tokyo High School principal and head of the Kodokan who renamed the school of jujitsu he founded as *judo*.[24] In this book, I use the

---

[23] The Chinese characters 一刀 are transliterated as *one sword*, or *ittō*, in Japanese. The suffix *ryu*, in this context, can be translated as *school* or *style*. Trans.

[24] Around this time, martial arts teachers in Japan started to replace the suffix *jutsu* with *dō* regarding the names of the martial arts they practiced to denote a more spiritual focus. Hence, jujitsu was renamed judo, kenjutsu was renamed kendo,

term *modern kendo* (*gendai kendo* 現代剣道) to refer to the sport of kendo that is recognized internationally. Since kenjutsu schools like the style of Ittō-ryū that I practice are sometimes called kendo by those not familiar with martial arts, when the terms *kenjutsu* and *kendo* appear in this book, I would like the reader to view them in a broader context of the traditional martial arts of Japan that did not include contests but were centered around practicing set patterns of movement called *kata*.

Within kenjutsu, what, specifically, does it mean to defeat an opponent? In the past, it meant to kill. But when

Figure 3: Students practicing Ono-ha Ittō-ryū at the Reigakudo dojo.

you look at the techniques of Ittō-ryū, I believe that this term has changed with the times to mean keeping your opponent from employing his fighting skills effectively. A specific example of how this might be done is by causing a serious injury to your opponent's right thumb, or the fist to which the thumb is attached, by stabbing or cutting. This is because once a person loses a thumb they cannot grasp a sword or use it, no matter how skilled they might be.

To defeat your opponent, Ittō-ryū teaches that you must go forward, no matter what. You will not know how strong your enemy is until you fight him, and the way to beat him is to take the initiative. There is a saying in Ittō-

---

etc. Trans.

ryū: "One is Victory, Two is Defeat" (*issho nihai* 一勝二敗). This means that if you take one action first you will win, but if your opponent comes forward to attack (one move) and you take action after avoiding it, your actions become two moves, in which case the side that is stronger will win. So even if you think you are about to lose or believe you are at some kind of disadvantage, you still have to move forward. The point is that moving forward is the key to winning. Though there are times we back up to draw the opponent toward us, we are not backing up to run away.

This is similar to the concept in modern kendo called *sen no sen* (先の先). This refers to defeating your opponent by seizing the initiative and attacking him first. But modern kendo also has the concept of *go no sen* (後の先), which means letting the opponent attack first then responding with an appropriate counter-attack. In Ittō-ryū, however, these different variations of taking the initiative are all taught as *taisen* (大先).

Simply rushing headlong to strike an opponent is unwise, so the concept of *going forward* includes not just moving yourself but also inducing your opponent to attack. By using facial expressions, slight movements, or threatening gestures, you can get your opponent to move or attack first. The advantage of this is that you will be able to cut into your opponent after getting some idea of how he will come toward you. We constantly keep this principle in mind when practicing. These are some things to consider when crossing swords with your adversary.

The Force That Knocks Away Everything

When someone cuts toward you, how is it possible to do kiriotoshi so that you avoid your opponent's blade and not get injured? We use the secret technique called *The Wheel Rolls Forward* (*sharin zenten* 車輪前転).

When a wheel or tire rotates while rolling forward, it generates enough power to knock away anything that comes into contact with it. But that happens only when there is a lot of momentum behind the tire and only when it rolls forward in a straight line. In Ittō-ryū, we propel ourselves forward like this wheel. By thinking of the hips as an axle and keeping the sword straight up and down as it rotates forward, everything moves in a circle around the hips. By doing this, you will be able to effortlessly cut straight into your opponent while, at the same time, easily deflect his blade to the side.

However, keeping the sword completely vertical while cutting is extremely difficult. Even if your posture is correct, if you lose your nerve, even a little, your sword blade will come down at an angle. To prevent this from happening, you must get rid of arrogance, indecisiveness, or weakness and cannot be concerned with winning or losing. We say this is "doing kiriotoshi to yourself." When a person achieves this level of mastery, they have achieved a mental state of not thinking about anything called *munen musō* (無念無想) but getting to that level is challenging. Ittōsai described this mental state as: "When a mosquito flies by your face, your hand moves to sweep it away without conscious thought. You should strive to develop the ability to wield a sword with this degree of unconscious effort." There are probably those who feel they can understand this intellectually but still worry about whether they can avoid being cut by not thinking about anything. Because this is one of the things I receive a lot of questions about, I would like to explain it in more detail.

To take a more contemporary explanation, you could say that to deflect your opponent's blade there is an angle at which the sword blades should meet, a speed at which they should move, and a certain spot where the blades should come together. You will eventually start to see these things if you train your eyes to. The professional baseball player, Ichiro,[25] can see a fastball as it is pitched toward him, judge where it will be, then hit it. But you don't need Ichiro's splendid ability of judging fastballs to practice kenjutsu because there are some tricks in Ittō-ryū you can use instead.

This was never explained in the past, but the secret to observing your opponent's movement is called *The Two Metsukes* (*futatsu no metsuke* 二つの目付) and refers to observing your opponent's entire body. When a person holding a sword starts to move, you can always see their initial movement. When they begin to raise their arms, their shoulders move just before their arms go up. Or when they think about striking your wrist, they will first glance at it. Their intention of *I think I will do this* is transmitted from their head, through their eyes, shoulders, arms, and finger tips, in that order, before they move. If you can spot those indicators, you need not fear your opponent. At the same time, you should train so that your opponent cannot read your intentions. Keep practicing until you can strike your opponent without conscious effort and without telegraphing your movements.

---

[25] New York Yankees professional baseball player, Suzuki Ichiro. In Japan he is simply known by his first name, *Ichiro*. Trans.

It is also important to wield the Japanese sword correctly. A katana has a sharp edge, a belly, angular sides, and a back. Because the edge of the blade will become nicked if it is used to stop an enemy's sword, we use the side or back of the sword when blocking or deflecting our opponent's blade. The blade of a katana is also curved. Those who practice modern kendo and only use the straight bamboo sword normally don't learn how to use a curved katana to smoothly deflect the blade of their opponent.

Ono-ha Ittō-ryū, Yagyū Shinkage-ryū, Tenshin Shōden Katori Shinto-ryū, Kashima Shinto-ryū, Heihō Niten Ichi-ryū…. these are among ten ancient kenjutsu schools listed in the table of contents of the book *Nihon no kenjutsu*[26] to which I was a contributor. I can say with confidence that there are no fundamental differences between the inner secrets of each of these traditions. They all resemble each other because they share the common purpose of teaching how to use the sword in actual conflict. That being the case, you may wonder why there are different schools of kenjutsu in the first place, and the reasons are due to differences between regions where they were created and popularized by famous swordsmen, differences in eras in which they evolved, and to differences in equipment they used. Some of these schools also incorporated other weapons, such as throwing stars and daggers, and a weapon combining a steel chain and sickle.

What would have happened if an expert in Ittō-ryū faced off against someone from one of these other schools? I will explain later how both Ittō-ryū and Shinkage-ryū were adopted as official fencing schools by the Tokugawa shogunate, but since they both served the Shogun,

---

[26] *Nihon no Kenjutsu* (Tokyo: Gakken Kenkyusha Inc., 2005)

members of each of these schools were prohibited from accepting challenges by other sword masters, so we will never know who would have come out ahead. I think it is safe to say, however, that the side that made the first cut would not have been beaten.

In addition, it is said that the Tokugawa shogunate never embraced other schools of kenjutsu because they considered these two to be superior to all others. Once Ittō-ryū was adopted, no other school of kenjutsu entered the service of the Shogun. I believe this is because there were no schools anywhere that could have defeated Ittō-ryū and Shinkage-ryū.

Learn All 170 and Then Go Back to One

From this point on I would like to introduce what we do when we train. Practice in Ittō-ryū conforms to the dictum passed down from Ittōsai: "All techniques start with the One Sword and return to the One Sword." Every Saturday, beginners practice from one forty-five to three o'clock P.M. After that, both beginners and advanced students train together until five o'clock. On Sundays, practice for advanced students only is held from three to five o'clock P.M.

When practicing, students wear a training uniform similar to what is worn in modern kendo but carry the wooden sword (*bokuto* 木刀) unique to Ittō-ryū. We do not wear protective masks. Instead, students are paired up where one student plays the role of *shikata*, the one who wins, (the student) and the other, *uchikata*, the one who loses, (the teacher). Uchikata wears a pair of protective gloves called *onigote* (鬼籠手) that are much thicker than those used in modern kendo. Then, as a pair, they practice the more than 170 techniques, one by one, which are divided into set patterns, or kata, that comprise the *kumitachi*. The kumitachi is the sum total of all of the techniques of Ono-ha Ittō-ryū, and the patterned movements within it teach students different ways of attacking as well as how to defend against someone else's attack. By practicing these techniques, over and over, the student learns how to move correctly, manipulate the sword effectively, and execute techniques skillfully.

I use the term *to strike* (*utsu* 打つ), but the meaning of *to strike* in modern kendo is quite different than in Ittō-ryū. In modern kendo, the wrist is used to lightly flick the bamboo sword to hit the opponent. This is because kendo is a competitive sport where the outcome of a match is determined by striking designated points on the body. In the case of Ittō-ryū, we carry a wooden sword that

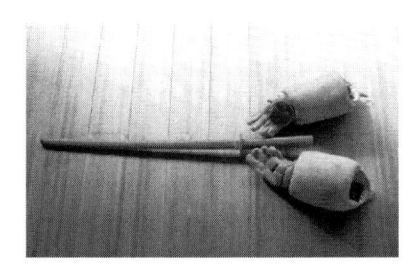

Figure 4: Onigote, training gloves used in Ittō-ryū, lying next to a wooden practice sword.

represents a katana. When we "strike" our opponent, we either use a cut called *oshikiru* (押し切る) in which the sword blade is pushed forward, across the target, or a cut called *hikikiru* (引き切る) in which the blade is drawn back across the target. We have to use the arms and elbows correctly to make these cuts effective. In addition to the targets common to modern kendo, such as the forehead, torso, and wrist, we also cut toward the neck. I also teach students to strike the forehead at the end of a technique as a *coup de grace*.

In the past, modern kendo enthusiasts used to mock the traditional schools of kenjutsu by saying things like, "These old styles [including Ittō-ryū] put too much emphasis on formality," but I would argue that the traditional schools provide a more logical and rational way to practice because they train to use real swords.

The uchikata wears leather onigote on both hands to absorb repeated blows from the shikata. These gloves are much thicker than boxing gloves and extend from the wrist to the elbow. They work well once you get used to them, but it can be quite painful when you first wear them and get hit.

The first technique a student learns within the curriculum of Ono-ha Ittō-ryū is called *One Victory* (*hitosugachi* 一ツ勝). This secret technique is the embodiment of kiriotoshi that I introduced in the beginning of this chapter. Once students are able to do this technique, they continue on to learn all 170 techniques of the remaining curriculum but then inevitably return to the very first technique of One Victory. When they finish this cycle, they gain a better understanding of the sword that was encapsulated in this first technique all along but which they did not notice at first. "Your starting point is your goal, your goal is your starting point" is what the *One* of One Victory really means.

The official crest of Ittō-ryū is based on this concept (see Figure 5). It is such a simple design that anyone can draw it. First, start with a point and trace a small circle in a clockwise direction, then, without lifting the pen off the paper, draw a straight, horizontal line toward the left. After that, pick a point and change directions, tracing a large circle around everything. When done, you create a design that completely encompasses both the small circle and the straight line. I would like to provide my interpretation of what this symbolizes.

Everything starts at a point. Extend this point out and it becomes a straight line; extend the line further and it becomes a circle. That original point represents oneself, and this crest symbolizes a form of personal development in which you do not limit yourself within the small circle

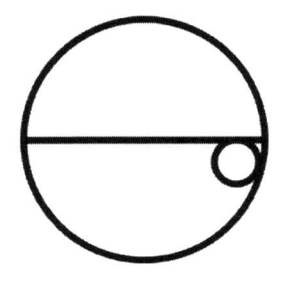

Figure 5: Ittō-ryū's official crest.

but expand beyond your personal limitations to achieve a level of development in which you comprehend fundamental truths that encompass the universe.

At first, new students should throw themselves into learning the technical aspects of Ittō-ryū, but as they progress they must go beyond that and think about the deeper implications and nuances of each technique. Learning the meaning and the logic of each and incorporating them into their training is an essential part of the educational process.

In Ittō-ryū, there are no competitions as in modern kendo. In our training, because we always teach students how to defeat their opponent, one partner is the winner and one is the loser. Also, we do not use bamboo swords but prefer wooden practice swords, and if we were to hit a practice partner with a wooden sword, it could cause death.

The Goal Is to Get Scrolls of Which Simply Stealing a Glance Was Strictly Prohibited

They say that, in the past, it took three years to master the first three techniques of the kumitachi and five years to master the first five. I consider it important for people to learn the full 170 techniques of the curriculum, though, so I try to teach the first five to ten within the first year. It is possible to learn everything within ten years, but most people can only learn up to twenty-five a year. So, how long does it take to learn all the techniques in the kumitachi? I believe that no matter how much you practice, it is never enough.

It is unfortunate he was not able to achieve his goal, but I recall when Kitajima Kosuke, the swimmer who attempted to win three gold medals in the London Olympics, was asked by a reporter before he left for England how far he would go, he answered, "There is no limit." When I heard that he felt that winning a gold medal was not his end goal, it made me think we share the same training philosophy and I wanted to support him even more.

Unlike modern kendo, Ittō-ryū does not have a promotion system based on rank gradations but uses a certificate system instead. There are three certificates, issued as scrolls called *mokuroku* (目録), and those who receive all three reach the rank of *menkyo kaiden* (免許皆伝), which means they are fully licensed to teach. The first scroll is the *Junikajō Mokuroku* (十二ヶ条目録), the second is the *Kanajishō Mokuroku* (仮名字書目録), and the third is the *Hon Mokuroku* (本目録). Names and diagrams of techniques are recorded in each of these scrolls, and, in the past, students would have been killed for just glancing at them. However, detailed descriptions of each technique are omitted. These details are transmitted orally from teacher to student, so it is impossible to learn the techniques just by reading them in a scroll. As a general rule, I issue the first scroll between the tenth and fifteenth year of training, if all goes well. While the training is simple and straightforward, I think that practicing Ono-ha Ittō-ryū offers students a unique experience.

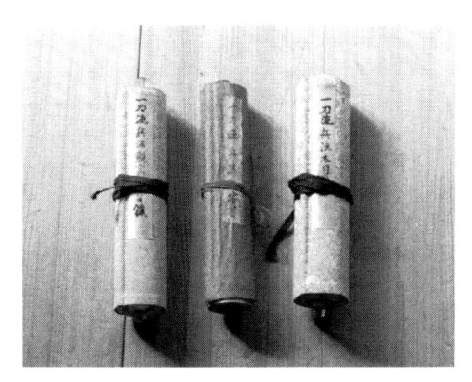

Figure 6: Scrolls issued as certificates of mastery in Ittō-ryū.

At first glance, this Way of the Sword seems tough but pursuing this path is gentle and easy-going. Being soft and blending with the movement of the opponent is also the idea behind the lesson of The Wheel Rolls Forward. In addition, the steps to achieve mastery are listed as: *shido, nyumon, shoshin, mijuku, jukuren, jotatsu, seimyō,* and *enman*.[27]

---

[27] The definitions of these terms are as follows: shido (志道) having the desire to begin training, nyumon (入門) turning that desire into action by entering the gate of the school, shoshin (初心) starting as a beginner, mijuku (未熟) advancing beyond beginner status to become a novice, jukuren (熟練) becoming more proficient than a novice and developing some level of skill, jotatsu (上達) constant improvement of skills, seimyō (精妙) further refinement of skills and knowledge, and enman(円満) achieving mastery by becoming well-rounded. Trans.

The door to our school is open to everyone, even beginners. We get visitors who already practice some other form of martial art as well as those who learned about Ittō-ryū through magazines or the Internet. Learning how to do Ittō-ryū has nothing to do with one's height and weight. Generally in sports, the bigger a person is, the more advantage they have, but, as in sumo, once a person grasps the logic behind the techniques he can defeat small and large opponents alike. Someone with good physical coordination will improve quickly, but relying on physical ability alone misses the point. Ittō-ryū is not suitable for those who demand immediate results, are impatient, or are overeager. The desire to make steady progress is all that is required.

Members of our school range in age from their twenties to their seventies but most are in their forties and fifties. In modern kendo, to which I have made comparisons many times, those in their thirties are unbeatable in competition. Due to rules that require competitors to engage in successive matches in which they need to score two points out of three within five minutes to win, physical strength and stamina are more important than anything else. But deciding the outcome of a fight with one cut of a sword has nothing to do with one's age. The more skilled you become in Ono-ha Ittō-ryū, the less you need power and speed. If you move your sword softly and in a circle, your opponent's sword that cuts toward you with brute force will merely bounce off.

In fact, there are experts in modern kendo who practice with us on a regular basis. As they moved up the ranks in kendo, they came to see the value of doing their sport with dignity and grace. When they first began kendo, they thought that it was okay to win even if it meant playing a little dirty, and they continued to practice that way for a long time. But the moment they realized something was wrong with that approach and decided they wanted to win cleanly, they decided to practice with us. Not surprisingly, learning the technique of kiriotoshi was their primary objective.

At present, the highest rank that can be earned in modern kendo is eighth degree. By the time those who pass the promotion exams advance to the rank of sixth, seventh, and eighth degree, they can execute a beautiful forehead strike (*shomen uchi* 正面打ち), which is the epitome of modern kendo techniques. Those who understand how to execute kiriotoshi can master this forehead strike in kendo much more easily. In fact, I have students in my school who also do kendo who opined that, "Before training in Ittō-ryū, I was afraid because I could not tell from which direction my opponent would strike, but once I became better at Ittō-ryū, I was able to. Even when I lost a match, I could understand why, whereas before practicing Ittō-ryū I could never tell." Getting rid of this fear was a major accomplishment for them. I also teach these concepts of Ittō-ryū to police officers during a twenty-hour intensive course at the National Police Academy (located in Fuchu, Tokyo) at the end of each year.

Foreigners, to include Americans, Italians, Germans, British, and Belgians, also practice at our dojo. They come from all walks of life, such as businesspeople, military service members from Yokota Air Base, and fire-fighters, but no matter what they do for a living, they are all very dedicated students.

People who have made the effort to learn Ittō-ryū maintain their composure while practicing. This is also a common trait among those who do modern kendo, and those with a good posture are more relaxed. When I see that I feel more at ease, too.

The Kenjutsu Instructor to the Tokugawa

This overview is rather long, but I would like to reintroduce the swordsman who came after the founder of Ittō-ryū. This was the military leader and sword master Mikogami Tenzen, later known as Ono Jiroemon Tadaaki, who succeeded Ittō Ittōsai as the second generation sōke of the tradition. He named the faction of Ittō-ryū he developed Ono-ha Ittō-ryū. The reason Mikogami was invited by Tokugawa Ieyasu to serve his son Hidetada is because Ono-ha Ittō-ryū was highly effective in actual combat. I will explain how this all came about below.

Before he was hired by the Shogun, Mikogami had declared that he was the "best swordsman among Heaven and Earth." Obata Kanbē Kagenori,[28] a samurai serving the Tokugawa shogunate as a military scholar, challenged him to a duel. Military scholars (*gunkakusha* 軍学者) are experts on military topics such as strategy and tactics. Obata was no match for Mikogami, and after he was soundly defeated became Mikogami's student. Shortly thereafter, Mikogami faced Yagyū Munenori, a master from the Yagyū Shinkage-ryū and fencing instructor to the Tokugawa

---

[28]Obata Kanbē Kagenori (小幡勘兵衛景憲) (1572-1663) was a Confucian scholar and retainer of the Takeda family during Japan's Sengoku period. He is perhaps best known for his completion of the *Koyo Gunkan*, the chronicle of the Takeda family's military campaigns. He created his own school of strategy called the *Kōshū-ryū Hiegaku*. Trans.

family, but Munenori was no match for him either. It was these two who recommended Mikogami to Ieyasu.

The story does not stop there, though. Around the same time, the chief of Hizaori Village (modern-day Asaka City, Saitama) rushed to Edo to appeal for help from the Shogun. "A swordsman named Onime murdered a member of our village and then locked himself in someone's house. We heard that a skilled sword master named Mikogami Tenzen was in Edo. We will not be able to resolve this situation on our own unless he comes to our village!" the chief pleaded.

Upon hearing this, Ieyasu ordered Mikogami to subdue the criminal and directed Obata to go along as an official inspector. When he arrived at the village, Mikogami challenged the bandit to a duel and cut off both of his arms no sooner than the fight started. Mikogami asked Obata, "Should I take his head?" and when Obata nodded his approval, Tenzen decapitated him with a single blow. Mikogami finished the job quickly and calmly while the nearby onlookers trembled with fear.

When Ieyasu received word of what had transpired, he elevated Mikogami to *hatamoto* status and employed him as the fencing instructor of his son Hidetada. After that, Hidetada bestowed a character from his own name on Mikogami, who incorporated it into his new name when he changed it to Ono Jiroemon Tadaaki.

The fencing schools Tokugawa Ieyasu employed remained unchanged until the restoration of imperial power, and, as I wrote earlier, the shogunate never adopted other schools of kenjutsu aside from Ono-ha Ittō-ryū and Yagyū Shinkage-ryū. But according to historical records, the role of the fifth generation headmaster, Ono Tadakata, evolved from providing actual instruction and training to the Shogun to merely performing martial arts exhibitions and demonstrations. This is because the threat of war was low and many warriors, including the Shogun, did not see the need to learn the art of the sword.

Around the same time, Ono-ha Ittō-ryū became entrenched within the domain of Tsugaru, which is how it came to be connected to my father, Sasamori Junzo. From here on, I will describe the flow of events that resulted in the migration of this school of kenjutsu from Edo to an area in the most northern part of mainland Japan.

The aforementioned Obata Kagenori played a prominent role in furthering the development of Ittō-ryū by becoming Ono Jiroemon Tadaaki's student and learning the school's full curriculum. One of Obata's students of military strategy was Yamaga Sokō (山鹿素行), a figure who developed his own school of strategic thought called *Yamaga-ryū Heihō* (山鹿流兵法). Yamaga, who was both a military strategist and Confucian scholar, gained notoriety for criticizing the orthodox Zhu Xi School of neo-Confucianism then staunchly supported by the shogunate. He was banished to the Akō Domain where his philosophy had a major influence on, among others, the famous Oishi Kuranosuke and his forty-seven *rōnin* of the Genroku Akō Incident.[29] From the time he arrived in Edo, many feudal

---

[29] This incident refers to a group of forty-seven masterless samurai (*rōnin*) who avenged the death of their feudal lord, Asano Naganori, after he was forced to commit ritual suicide for attacking a court official named Kira Yoshinaka within the precinct of the Shogun's castle. Believing that Asano was bullied and humiliated to the point that he had no choice but to assault Kira for the sake of his honor, the rōnin waited for a year while plotting their revenge under the leadership of Oishi Kuranosuke. After they attacked and killed Kira in his mansion, they

lords sought to learn Yamaga-ryū Heihō from him and were heavily influenced by his philosophy. Among them was Tsugaru Nobumasa, the Lord of the Tsugaru Domain.

This association led to Ono Tadaaki teaching Ono-ha Ittō-ryū to the strategist Obata and his pupil Yamaga Sokō. In return, Ono Tadaaki learned the *Kōshū-ryū Heigaku* (甲州流兵学) system of strategy from Obata. Thereafter, the leaders of Tsugaru who came together to study under Yamaga Sokō ended up learning both the Yamaga-ryū Heihō system of strategy and Ono-ha Ittō-ryū. Due to this interchange, Ono Tadaaki and his descendants established a foundation of personal connections with Tsugaru Nobumasa and his descendants that ultimately facilitated the migration of Ittō-ryū from the capital city of Edo to the Tsugaru Domain.

Tsugaru Nobumasa enthusiastically studied Ono-ha Ittō-ryū and eventually received the secrets of the school from the fourth generation headmaster, Ono Tadao. His successor, Nobuhisa, likewise mastered the secrets of the school from Tadao. Because both generations of daimyo mastered Ittō-ryū, the samurai of the Tsugaru Domain, both those serving in Edo and those remaining in Tsugaru,[30] began to study it en-masse.

---

submitted themselves to the shogunate and were forced to commit ritual suicide for the crime of murder. Eventually, the loyalty and perseverance of these men became legend, and this story has become a recurring theme in both traditional and contemporary culture. Trans.

[30] Under Tokugawa rule, feudal lords were forced to maintain official residences both in their home domains as well as the capital city of Edo. Trans.

The Next Headmaster Is My Lord

Around this time, headmasters of martial arts schools were bestowing the leadership of their factions on daimyo[31] and temporarily giving them the title of sōke, and then later returning that title back to their own households. Disciples were officially recognized as successors of the school after they were conferred special documents, called *densho* (伝書), in which the doctrine and techniques of the school were recorded. Alternating the leadership of the school between a daimyo family member and the head of a martial arts household also served the purpose of raising the profile of the school by capitalizing on the prestige and influence of the feudal lord. The title of sōke was passed back and forth between the Lord of Owari and the Yagyū family even within the Yagyū Shinkage-ryū.

In the case of Ono-ha Ittō-ryū, from the founder Ittō Ittōsai until the fifth generation headmaster, the sōke-ship of the school remained within the Ono household. The fifth sōke, Ono Tadakazu, conferred all of the school's secrets to Tsugaru Nobuhisa, who was then the Lord of Tsugaru, so that he could pass on the leadership of the school to Ono Tadakazu's son Tadahisa. But something unexpected happened. Just after Tadahisa completed his full initiation from Nobuhisa with the anticipation of becoming the next sōke, he died suddenly, and his son Tadakata was not yet an adult. So, after Tsugaru Nobuhisa, who had since retired, once again passed on the secrets of Ittō-ryū to Tadakata, the lineage of the school returned to the Ono family. As a result, the manner in which the

---

[31] Daimyo were large hereditary land owners, second in political power only to the ruling Shogun. Trans.

leadership of the school was transferred back and forth between these families ended up saving the Ono faction of Ittō-ryū. If the true teaching of this school had not passed between the Ono and Tsugaru families, it is possible that the Ono branch of Ittō-ryū would have died out.

Although the Lord of Tsugaru himself became the sōke, it is unlikely that a person with his social status would have taught or provided guidance directly to students. His position in the social hierarchy was firmly established, and it would have been unthinkable for a feudal lord to teach his retainers in this way. It was the Yamaga family that took on the responsibility of doing the actual instructing and ended up serving as the connection between the Lord of Tsugaru and the students learning Ittō-ryū.

As stated earlier, Tsugaru Nobumasa had longed to study under the strategist Yamaga Sokō and was later succeeded by his son Nobuhisa, who was also fully initiated into Ittō-ryū. Though Nobumasa tried his best to get Sokō to relocate to Tsugaru, Yamaga sent his adopted son, Okinobu, instead. After that, successive generations of the Yamaga family served the House of Tsugaru by teaching both Ittō-ryū and the Yamaga-ryū Heihō system of strategy. After this structure evolved, Ono-ha Ittō-ryū became firmly entrenched within the Tsugaru Domain.

The Major *Katanashi* Trend in Kenjutsu

Aside from the Ono branch, many other factions grew out of Ittō-ryū. One that became popular in Edo was called the Nakanishi. This branch developed a practice sword made from four strips of bamboo that spurred on the growth of modern kendo. From the very beginning of Ittō-ryū, a bamboo practice sword called a *fukuroshinai* (袋竹刀) that was fashioned from thirty two strips of bamboo and covered in a cloth bag was used alongside the wooden practice sword. The Nakanishi branch made major refinements in the equipment they used, such as modifying the bamboo sword of Ittō-ryū and creating facemasks and other protective gear similar to what is used in kendo today. The Nakanishi Dojo became famous for making these innovations.

It is not difficult to imagine that doing such things as competing with bamboo swords while wearing protective armor was more fun than practicing the rigid patterns of kata. This method of training became more and more popular starting from the end of the Bakumatsu period and was called *gekken*, as I noted previously.

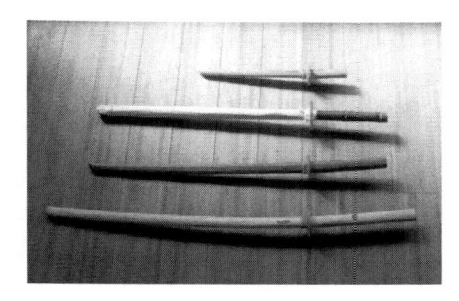

Figure 7: The practice swords of Ittō-ryū. The fukuroshinai is second from the top.

The kenjutsu old guard raised their eyebrows at this new trend, though. Correspondence between the Yamaga family in Tsugaru and the Nakanishi family in Edo remains. Contained in these letters are heated exchanges such as, "The young people of today do nothing but compete against each other with bamboo swords and do not practice kata. This is *katanashi kenjutsu*.[32]" From these exchanges, the term *katanashi* came to mean such things as "to lose face" and "to become thoroughly useless."

---

[32] Literally, kenjutsu without kata. Trans.

Hoksuhin Ittō-ryū, which was practiced by Sakamoto Ryōma, evolved from the Nakanishi branch of Ittō-ryū. Also, Asari Yoshinobu, one of the top instructors of the Nakanishi branch, taught Yamaoka Tesshū,[33] a retainer of the Shogun. Later, Yamaoka became the top student in Ono-ha Ittō-ryū and reviewed and copied the densho and other secret documents that the ninth-generation sōke, Ono Nario, showed him. He declined to take over as the head of the school, however, creating another faction instead that he named Ittō Shōden Mutō-ryū (一刀正伝無刀流).

So how did the orthodox school of Ono-ha Ittō-ryū come to be transmitted to my father, Sasamori Junzo, the sixteenth sōke? My grandfather, Sasamori Yozo, held such posts for the Tsugaru Domain as Chief Master-at-Arms while he was in Hirosaki, and as Commander of the Household Guards who protected the Lord of Tsugaru when he served in Edo. He excelled in the martial arts, the spear in particular. Junzo was born in 1886 as his youngest son. Starting as a small child, my father practiced Ittō-ryū at a local dojo in Hirosaki called the Hokushindō (北辰堂). The master who taught at this dojo was the official kenjutsu instructor of the former Tsugaru Domain.

Junzo continued to be active in the martial arts when he attended the Aomori Prefecture First Middle School (currently Hirosaki High School). While there, he

---

[33] Both Sakamoto Ryōma and Yamaoka Tesshū were pivotal figures during the Meiji Restoration. Ryōma is famous for, among other things, cementing an alliance between the Tōsa and Chōshū Domains that opposed the ruling Bakufu, and Tesshū was noted for negotiating the surrender of Edo castle to imperial forces led by Saigo Takamori, thereby sparing the city and its civilian inhabitants from needless bloodshed. Trans.

continued to train under the guidance of a martial arts master and Ono-ha Ittō-ryū expert named Nakahata Hidegoro. He also practiced modern kendo, and after he graduated and entered Waseda University, became captain of the school's kendo club. In 1909 he took first place at the All Japan Youth Kendo Championship.

After graduating from college, he travelled to America where he continued his studies and established the North American Budo Association. He organized several exhibition matches that helped spread the popularity of judo and kendo in the United States. While sailing home on the Oriental Steamer *Korea-maru*, he met Tokugawa Iesato, then returning to Tokyo after representing Japan at

Figure 8: Sasamori Junzo prepared for kendo practice.

the Washington Naval Conferences on arms reductions. It appears they discussed Ittō-ryū on the voyage. I have calligraphy in my home written by Iesato with the term *ruro muge* (流露無碍) (don't stop; execute techniques continuously)—one of the secrets of Ittō-ryū—written inside.

As I will discuss in the following chapters, after returning to Japan, Junzo became both the principal of the Tō-ōgijuku (東奥義塾) in Hirosaki, the Tsugaru Domain's main educational institute, and the chancellor of Aoyama Gakuin in Tokyo. At no point in his travels, however, did he neglect to practice the Way of the Sword. He always felt he needed to faithfully present Ono-ha Ittō-ryū to the world.

Junzo was forty years old when he became the sōke of Ono-ha Ittō-ryū, which is around the same time he became principal of the Tō-ōgijuku. At that time, a man named Yamaga Motojiro was between the Ono and Tsugaru families and the next in line from the Yamaga family to become the sōke of Ono-ha Ittō-ryū. A graduate of the Tō-ōgijuku, he worked hard to revitalize his alma mater and later even became a trustee of the school. Motojiro was a Christian minister and decided not to pursue the path of kenjutsu, so in 1926, he presented my father, with whom he had a connection through the Tō-ōgijuku, with all the various transmission scrolls of the school, to include an official teaching license (*shinan menjō* 指南免状).

Moreover, the sōke within the Tsugaru family at that time was Tsugaru Yoshitaka. He was the father of Her Imperial Highness, The Princess Hitachi. Yoshitaka and my father were acquaintances, and when my father succeeded Yamaga Motojiro as the head of Ittō-ryū, Yoshitaka presented him with the secret initiation materials (*gokui kaiden* 極意皆伝), oral teachings (*kuden* 口伝 and *kikigaki* 聞書), secret transmission scrolls (*gokui densho* 極意伝書), and all other written documents.

After the Meiji era, though both the Tsugaru and Yamaga families had the authority to issue licenses in Ittō-ryū, the fact is that neither continued to practice the art. So, after all the written transmissions scrolls and other documents were transferred to Junzo, he became the sixteenth sōke of Ono-ha Ittō-ryū. After that, he inherited the Shinmusō Hayashizaki-ryū school of iaidō and the Chokugen-ryū school of naginata that had been transmitted within the Tsugaru Domain from their respective headmasters as well.

Aside from these, one other Way that Junzo faithfully pursued from when he was a child was Christianity.

Chapter 4

Hearts Filled with Both Bushido and Christianity

The Faith That a True Samurai Brought Home

Around the time of the birth of my father, Sasamori Junzo, members of the Sasamori family had been steadily converting to Christianity. In this chapter, after first describing how Christianity spread to the Tsugaru area, I would like to discuss how Junzo came to follow the paths of both Christianity and the martial arts.

The man who played the biggest role as a Christian evangelist in the Tsugaru Domain was Honda Yoichi (1849-1912). He was of the same generation as Nitobe and Uchimura and later became the Chancellor of Aoyama Gakuin, a prominent Christian school in Tokyo. The Honda family that served the Tsugaru Domain traced its lineage to the Hondas that had served the Tokugawa for generations. The Hondas first came to Tsugaru when Tokugawa Ieyasu's adopted daughter Matehime (満天姫) married into the Tsugaru family. The Hondas became a prominent family serving the domain as senior retainers.

Honda Yoichi had a reputation for academic brilliance from boyhood, and by the time he was seven years old had mastered such Chinese classics as the *Analects of Confucius*. He was able to read the texts in their original Chinese and recite them aloud in proper Japanese without any study aids. At the age of thirteen, he also began to learn Ono-ha Ittō-ryū, which was then being taught within the Tsugaru Domain. He was so recognized for his brilliance and ability that he was promoted to the head of the class in the domain's main training academy, the Keikokan, by the time he was sixteen.

In 1868, the Boshin War broke out and the Tsugaru supported the shogunate. Honda was sent on a diplomatic mission to cement a military alliance with the Shōnai

Figure 9: Honda Yoichi

Domain in order to strengthen the Ōuetsu Reppan Alliance (奥羽越列藩同盟) which had formed to oppose the Imperial Army led by the Satsuma and Chōshū. He successfully obtained from the Shōnai a ship and several hundred muskets but returned home only to find that, at the eleventh hour, the Tsugaru had switched sides and now supported the forces loyal to the Emperor.

The instigator of this switch was a samurai named Nishidate Kosei. A visionary who was able to foresee the dawning of a new era, he was posted in Kyoto as the official representative of the Tsugaru and oversaw the domain's Kyoto Mansion, a type of official residence each domain maintained in Kyoto, which is centered in western Japan close to Osaka. Nishidate collected intelligence from the Imperial Guards and the House of Hosokawa, and concluded that the reign of the Tokugawa Bakufu had come to an end. He sent a detailed report that convinced the Lord of Tsugaru to switch his allegiance to the Imperial faction.

Upon hearing of this decision, Honda asked the Lord of Tsugaru to allow him to commit ritual suicide as a way of apologizing to the Shōnai for this betrayal. The one who stopped him from doing this was Nishidate. Honda, along with his close friend Kikuchi Kurō, then deserted the Tsugaru and proceeded to the Shōnai where they joined forces with them to fight alongside the Tokugawa forces.

After the fall of the Shōnai, Nishidate decided to spare the life of the able Honda, forgave him the offense of deserting the domain, and called him back to serve without uttering a word. This is because the elders of the Tsugaru Domain, and even the daimyo himself, were impressed by the loyalty and sincerity of Honda, the man who, as a youth, had distinguished himself in both literature and the martial arts.

A Chinese Language Bible Obtained in Secret

Honda, like many of his contemporary samurai, followed the teachings of Wang Yangming. As described previously, the doctrine of this school emphasized the precept, "knowing but not acting is the same as not knowing," which is another way of saying it emphasized the practical.

At the same time, he encountered another philosophy that changed his life. This was Christianity. In 1869 he secretly obtained a Chinese language translation of the

Bible from China. Although Shinto had countless gods, there was but one God in the Bible, and Honda was surprised to read that that this one God created all things. It would be four more years before the ban on learning Christianity would be lifted, so Honda was forced to read the Bible in secret.

Later, Honda was sent to Yokohama from Tsugaru to study under the Christian missionary James Ballagh. While there, he became one of the Yokohama Band that studied in Ballagh's school, the Ballagh Juku. As noted earlier, the encouragement of many young people to study under foreigners who arrived in Japan during the beginning of the Meiji era gave birth to one of the three great Protestant movements in Japan.

At first, Honda had no intention to convert to Christianity, but Ballagh's charismatic personality won him over. A short time later, he lost his support from the Tsugaru as a live-away student and had to return to his home when the old feudal domains were abolished and replaced by the modern prefectural system. He raised money by selling off his estate, and then returned to Yokohama where he resumed his studies in the Ballagh Juku. The next year he was baptized and became a Christian. When he was baptized, Honda had this to say:

> Mr. Ballagh was full of the spirit of mission work. I had never been that moved before and admired that spirit. I admired his passion. He allowed us to be treated as samurai. Around 1872 we were taking a great risk...At that time, Ballagh said, "You are in danger. But even if you are arrested, you must not become disaffected toward your country. Disciples of Christ must obey the laws of their country. There

is a way to avoid them in America, but this is not the spirit of Christianity. Resolve yourself to be condemned to banishment in accordance with the laws of your country, wherever you are." When we heard this, we knew Dr. Ballagh truly came to Japan for the sake of our country, our desire to expel foreigners disappeared, and, instead, we felt that we needed to get him to stay.[34]

After his baptism, Honda returned to Tsugaru and became devoted to spreading Christianity. When he returned, he saw that the Keikokan, the school where he had studied as a youth, had closed when the feudal domains were abolished. Honda, along with Kikuchi Kurō, his friend with whom he had deserted the Tsugaru Domain and who was studying at the Keiōgi Juku,[35] went to work to reorganize the school. Receiving financial support from the Tsugaru family, they reconstructed the school in 1872 as a private institution and named it Tō-ōgijuku. (This school still exists as Tō-ōgijuku Junior-Senior High School).

The name of the school is said to have come from Kikuchi's close friend, Fukuzawa Yukichi. While discussing the idea of building the new school, Fukuzawa suggested that since the school would be located deep in the East of Japan, they should call it the Tō-ōgijuku. The school also copied the curriculum of the Keiōgi Juku. The first headmaster of the school was the principal who had previously been in charge of the Keikokan, but he was

---

[34] Collected works of Saba Wataru, *Uemura Masahisa to Sono Jidai*, Volume 1.
[35] This later became Keio University, which was founded by Fukuzawa Yukichi. Trans.

succeeded by Kikuchi. Honda eventually replaced Kikuchi at Kikuchi's request.

The Connection between the Missionary Named Ing and Apples

The faculty at the Tō-ōgijuku enthusiastically worked to introduce Western learning to Aomori. A year after the school opened, an American couple, the Wolfs, started to teach English there, becoming the first English teachers in Tohoku. A year later they resigned and an American missionary named John Ing (1840-1910) arrived. Ing held the rank of major in the Union cavalry during the American Civil War and had taken his family to China to head a Methodist mission there, but when a member of his family fell ill he decided to return home. When his ship pulled into the port of Yokohama on the return leg of his voyage, Ballagh happened to introduce him to Honda Yoichi. Though still grieving over the loss of his daughter who had died shortly after childbirth, he was impressed by Honda's enthusiasm and followed him to Hirosaki.

Ing turned out to be an excellent teacher. He revised the curriculum of the Tō-ōgijuku, introducing English language textbooks that covered, aside from English, natural history, mathematics, science, and history. It is doubtful that the students understood all of the lessons because they were in English, but it is recorded that they were deeply moved by his sermons.

Due to the influence of Ing and Honda, the number of people who became interested in Christianity began to increase, starting with members of the former samurai class. In less than a year, fifteen young men decided to be baptized. This trend can be likened to what happened at

Sapporo Agricultural College. Consequently, the Tō-ōgijuku became the center of Christian evangelism in Aomori.

Because a church was needed to perform a baptismal ceremony, a non-denominational church was to be constructed in Hirosaki in 1875. The Church of Christ in Yokohama, the church to which Honda first belonged, was in principle a non-denominational Protestant church, but Ing was a missionary of the Methodist faith, which is Protestant, so after first obtaining permission from the church in Yokohama, he turned the non-denominational church planned for Hirosaki into a Methodist Church. In one stroke, this decision created Japan's first Protestant Church founded by Japanese and Japan's first Methodist Church in the Tohoku region.

The Methodist denomination was formed in the eighteenth century by the brothers John and Charles Wesley, who started out as members of the Church of England. At the time, the English aristocracy was in social turmoil, and no matter how famous the university, students lived a life of luxury, did nothing but attend parties, were late for class, and neglected their studies. The Wesley brothers were attending university in that environment and advocated a lifestyle that followed certain rules (Methods) which, in practice, lead to spiritual purification. Thus they were nicknamed "Methodists" (they were also called the Holy Club). This is the origin of the name of the denomination. They believed that applying religious principles to their daily lives made their faith real. Unlike the Presbyterian Church, which is also Protestant but takes a theoretical approach to deepening one's understanding of one's faith and which is sometimes called the *denomination of theory*, Methodism is called the *denomination of action.* The difference between these two is very much like the difference between the schools of Confucianism advocated by Zhu Xi and Wang Yangmin.

In the three years and four months of Ing's short stay in Japan, he left more in Tsugaru than merely his faith. Because there were often food shortages in northern Japan, Ing imported seeds and seedlings for eggplant, cabbage, asparagus, tomatoes, and apples and taught local farmers how to cultivate them. You cannot find them much anymore, but at one time there was a breed of apple famous in Aomori called the *Indo Apple*. One theory about how this variety of apple got its name is that the seedlings were named after Ing when he imported them, but local people mispronounced his name, calling the trees *Indo* rather than *Ing*. Another explanation is that he imported the seedlings from his home state of Indiana, so the apples were originally called *Indiana Apples*, and this was later shortened to *Indo Apples*. Either way, there is no doubt that these apples can be traced back to him.

Also, Ing's wife had a big impact on the students, and she was adored for the motherly affection she showed for them. One winter she decorated a Christmas tree, gathered the students around it, and likely held Japan's first-ever Christmas service. When it finally became time for the Ings to leave, the students transported her in a palanquin while they themselves walked in the falling snow with only sandals on their feet. While the Ings were in Hirosaki, the number of people baptized reached thirty five.

Honda Yoichi said of the Ings:

> In order to obtain an understanding of Christianity, reading books and listening to lectures by scholars is good, but even more important is to experience

the impact of a living witness who has led a rich spiritual life. The work of the missionaries is the work of God, and coming into personal contact with them and other spiritual leaders is how you come to really know your faith.

Incidentally, Honda later became a minister of the Hirosaki Church and also served as a member of the Aomori Prefectural Assembly. He later travelled to America and, upon his return, became the second principal of the Tokyo English-Japanese School, which had been established by Methodist missionaries. In 1894, this school changed its name to Aoyama Gakuin, and Honda also served there as the school's second chancellor.

Converting to Christianity Was More Difficult Than Cutting Off His Topknot

Christianity took root in the Tsugaru area largely due to proselytizing by Ing and Honda, and this is how the Sasamori family came in contact with it. My uncle Sasamori Uichiro, the eldest son of my grandfather, Sasamori Yozo, attended the Tō-ōgijuku and was later baptized at the Hirosaki Church due to the influence of Honda Yoichi. He was the first of the Sasamori family to become a Christian. Along with Honda, he was also intimately involved in the Freedom and People's Rights Movement.[36] My grandmother was also baptized. She was

---

[36] The Freedom and People's Rights Movement (*jiyuminken undo* 自由民権運動), was a political and social movement that promoted democratic principles, such as democratically elected local and national assemblies and the creation of a Western-style

my grandfather's second wife, and together they had my father, Junzo, who was my grandfather's youngest child. Junzo recalled hearing Bible stories while being bounced on his mother's knee and concluded that it was only natural that he would come to believe in God.

Figure 10: Sasamori family photo. Sasamori Yozo is seated front row, third from left. His son Uichiro is seated to his left. Junzo is the teenage boy in the second row, third from right. The Imperial Army officer in the front row, far right, is Yozo's son Asada Ryoitsu, who was adopted by the Asada family.

As noted before, the Methodist denomination is very devout and strictly prohibited smoking and drinking. In the latter half of the nineteenth century, the United States passed laws prohibiting the sale of alcohol, and the Methodists played a central role in getting those laws adopted. My grandfather loved to drink sake and also

---

constitution. Trans.

lived in an era when the retainers of the Tsugaru Domain wore their hair in the traditional topknot – the distinct mark of a samurai. He used to say that when he converted to Christianity it was tougher for him to give up drinking than to cut off his topknot. Nevertheless, members of the Sasamori family have been Christians ever since.

These rules may have been very strict; however, I cannot help but think that once these former samurai adopted the Christian faith they started to see the commonalities between Christianity and Bushido. When these warriors had been serving their feudal lords, they believed that they would become no better than commoners if they did not maintain the Spartan lifestyle of a samurai. When their world underwent such a momentous political change during the Meiji Restoration and they no longer served a daimyo, they seemed to have turned to Christianity to fill the void.

One group that was wary about the spread of Christianity throughout the Tsugaru area was the Buddhists. My father said that, when he was a teenager, Christian ministers and Buddhist priests used to have religious debates in public. My father took part in these debates and recalled that the audience tended to side with the Christian point of view. However, my father personally always respected the Buddhist and Shinto faiths, which are part of the traditional culture of Japan.

Support for Christianity started to grow ever stronger in Tsugaru. This was attributed to, in no small part, the egalitarian spirit which lies at the heart of Christianity. Though Japan had entered the Meiji era, the Tsugaru region, not to mention the rest of Japan, still had a stratified society. The citizenry were no longer required to register as one of the four official social classes of warrior, farmer, artisan, and merchant, but a sense of class distinction still lingered among the populace. Visitors who went to worship at the Hirosaki Church, however, found themselves standing next to former samurai, farmers, artisans, and merchants, all gathered together in fellowship under the same roof. This was a big shock to all who attended.

Figure 11: Hirosaki Methodist Church today.

Missionaries, students of the Tō-ōgijuku, and parishioners from local Christian churches also visited communities of those who had been ostracized from society and conducted educational activities there, including teaching them about the Bible. The church even opened a night school to help educate young people serving in what can best be described as a form of indentured servitude to help them open small businesses and live more independently. The people of Tsugaru became more and more amazed at these types of activities, and the number of those interested in Christianity started to increase.

Chapter 5

Looks Can Be Deceiving

Kindness on the Battlefield

When I was born in Tsugaru in 1933 as the youngest of Sasamori Junzo's three sons, it was natural for both Christianity and Bushido, centered on Ittō-ryū, to coexist within our household. My father was a very kind person, but also very strict and hated when things were not right. When we did something wrong, he would not hesitate to let us know in a firm manner. Looking back at it, our lifestyle was very similar to that of a samurai's, and from an early age I came to have a strong interest in Bushido. Even as a child I always felt it was something important.

My mother's side of the family also came from samurai lineage. My maternal grandfather was a vassal of the Shimazu and skilled in the Jigen-ryū school of kenjutsu, which was commonly taught within the Satsuma Domain. After fighting in the Boshin War, he entered the Imperial Army and eventually rose to the rank of lieutenant general, served as a Division Commander, and was later appointed as a baron. In 1877, he participated in the Russo-Turkish war as a military attaché accompanying the Imperial Russian Army and played a role in the liberation of Bulgaria when the Russians drove the Ottoman-Turkish army out of that country. To this day a monument erected in his honor still stands in Bulgaria.

While working as a Japanese language teacher, my mother used to tell me stories about the great leaders of the *Heike Monogatari* and the Sengoku period. The story of Kimura Shigenari made a particular impression on me.

As a vassal of Toyotomi Hideyori, Shigenari was a very gentle man and familiar with court etiquette. From the outside he looked rather weak. An arrogant monk named Miyoshi Seikai Nyudo, one of the Ten Heroes of Sanada, accosted Shigenari one day saying, "Why does Lord Hideyori think so highly of someone such as you?" When Shigenari let his guard down, Nyudo jumped forward and attacked. Shigenari extended one hand and pinned him to the floor in a flash. With that one motion, Nyudo was immobilized. This action stunned Nyudo, and he gained great respect for Shigenari.

Though I committed to memory the story my mother related, I don't know where it came from and it wasn't until I became an adult and learned similar empty-handed techniques in Ittō-ryū that I really believed it could be true. The lessons I learned from my mother were that those who look strong and tough are not necessarily so, and that those who are kind and gentle can also be really strong.

I have also never forgotten the story of "The Death of Atsumori" from the *Heike Monogatari*. Near the end of the Genpei campaign, Atsumori of the Taira clan was trying to flee to safety when Kumagai Naozane of the Minamoto clan called for him to stop and challenged him to single combat. Just as Kumagai was about to take Atsumori's head, he hesitated after seeing that Atsumori was a mere lad around the same age as his own teenage son. Though he wanted to find a way to let him go, Kumagai's fellow samurai were bearing down on the both of them and they would surely kill Atsumori themselves if he did not.

Recognizing this, Atsumori said, "There is no way my life can be spared. I would like you to do the honor." Kumagai reasoned that at least the boy would die by his hand and he could pray for the boy's soul later, so he took Atsumori's head. This story presents an example of how those who followed the Bushido code never lost their compassion, even on the battlefield. Therefore, to me, Bushido, rather than being a philosophy in which you come to understand through logical thought or by reading special books, is something you master through what you do in your daily life, which includes practicing Ittō-ryū.

At the same time, I was attracted to Christianity. The kindergarten I attended, like nearly all kindergartens in Hirosaki, was in a Christian school, and I remember being mesmerized by the beauty of the Christian hymns our teacher sang to us while she played the organ.

During those days of both physical and spiritual training, my father became the Principal of the Tō-ōgijuku. Prior to his taking up this post, the school had not been managed very well, and it closed in 1913 due to financial difficulties. There were calls to reopen the school, however, and support was provided by Hirosaki City as well as the Methodist Episcopal Church in America, then celebrating the 100-year anniversary of the missionary John Wesley. The Tō-ōgijuku reopened in 1922 at the request of the church, and my father assumed the duty as the first principal. Both kendo and Christianity were included as compulsory subjects. Shortly thereafter, as explained in Chapter 3, he became the 16th-generation Sōke of Ittō-ryū.

In 1939, at the age of 53, my father accepted a job as Chancellor of Aoyama Gakuin, a Methodist school in Tokyo, and I started a new life in the capital. I was six years old when I entered the kindergarten there. Gradually, the specter of war loomed ever larger and our family steadfastly defended our faith in Christianity. Because of this, my father was harassed by the high-handed military leadership of Japan, who had become increasingly critical of my father's Christian teaching, and he was left with no choice but to stand up to this bullying.

The Chancellor of Aoyama Gakuin Under Surveillance by the Military

Japanese military authorities before the war were convinced there were spies among the many foreign missionaries working in Christian schools throughout Japan. Reportedly, they placed the faculty members of Aoyama Gakuin, Doshisha University, and Meiji Gakuin under surveillance. The schools themselves were run thanks to American donations, so the authorities took advantage of whatever opportunities they could to close them down. They dispatched soldiers to each school and tried to stop religious services as well as institute military-style training. My father opposed this, protesting that since the schools were not military organizations they should not be forced to make students perform military drills and ceremonies. My father was a Christian but was still involved in kendo and Ittō-ryū. And since he was a man of the Meiji era, he paid his respects to the Emperor and even visited Shinto shrines. Though he had great respect for the Emperor, he always maintained his belief that there was only one God.

Around this time a major incident occurred. The year before the Pacific War started, a man named Baker who represented the World Council of Churches (WCC, headquartered in Geneva), the largest Protestant organization in the world, and one other missionary visited Japan. They met with then-Foreign Minister Matsuoka Yōsuke in an effort to convince him to prevent further conflict. I don't if know they delivered the same Christian point of view to the United States government, and I suppose their message could also have come from the United States, but my father was the one who brought the two parties together. As far as he was concerned, he just wanted to avoid war. His older brother was a lieutenant general in the Imperial Army, held the title of Baron, and was serving as a Regimental Commander of the Imperial Guards. After getting an update about the military situation from him, my father took on the job of intermediary between the WCC representatives and the Foreign Minister.

In the meeting, after Baker said that Japan should refrain from invading China and Manchuria, Matsuoka did not give any ground but flatly replied, "America, in particular, should stay out of this affair." He then went even further, emphasizing that foreigners residing in Japan should go home, and an order to expel all foreign residents from Japan was eventually issued. There were hundreds of missionaries all over Japan at the time. I heard my father tell the story of how he saw off the last one to depart Yokohama saying, "Soon, we will probably be at war. We will each do our best on behalf of our own countries."

Since my father opposed the war, you may wonder about the safety of my family. We were never directly threatened, but we were kicked out of our house and lost our home. At the time, we lived in a house owned by family on my mother's side located near the Akasaka

Imperial Army base. Once when I went to the foyer, a soldier was there.

"There appear to be empty rooms in this house, so we would like you to let us use them to house some officers," he said.

Childishly, I was in awe and thought it was cool, but my father was very upset. He sent the officer away, explaining that the house was a civilian residence and that military officials were not welcome to live there. Sure enough, we were soon forced to relocate as a result of this discussion. It was a forced eviction. The authorities told us that if there was a fire it would be very hazardous. The house was torn down shortly thereafter. Right next to it was a house that belonged to a brigadier general in the Imperial Army, but that was how it was back then. We had no place to live, so my father moved into a row house nearby, and my brother, sister, and I moved back to Hirosaki.

The military authorities continued to ratchet up the pressure on Aoyama Gakuin by trying to draft the students into military units. My father argued that since the students at the school were extremely talented, they should be commissioned as officers. However, when the military threatened that if the Chancellor did not quit they would send all the young men conscription papers enlisting them as privates and take further action to close down the school itself, he had no choice but to resign from his post for the sake of the students and the future of the school. The author Kiyosawa Kiyoshi recorded in his book *Ankoku nikki* that around this time there was a fight over each position within the school.

"That Cross Is Not Mine"

My brother, sister, and I started life in Hirosaki as wartime evacuees. I will never forget one day when I was in the fifth grade. I invited a friend to my house and when I brought out one of my favorite toys to show him, a cross accidently came out with it. It was a cross I got from my mother, and my friend saw it. He didn't say anything, but when I went to school the next morning a hall monitor from the sixth grade was standing at the entrance of the school and spotted me. "So you are a Christian, huh? Amen, somen,[37] eh?" he said. During the war, Christians felt as if they had to keep a low profile, even in Hirosaki where Christianity had previously taken root. The sixth grader continued, "Christianity is a religion from an enemy country, so you can't come into the school." Because I was a wartime evacuee from Tokyo, bullying me would always be easy. I didn't like this, so I lied and said that the cross was not mine to get him to let me in.

That day, after I returned home, I opened the Bible and happened to come across the story of the early Christians who were persecuted for following their beliefs. After reading about their experiences, I became ashamed of my earlier actions. The next day I announced to my friends, "I am a Christian." After that, the bullying really started.

After publicly proclaiming my faith, I was more determined than ever to support the church that I had turned my back on before. The missionaries from the West were gone due to the edict evicting foreigners, so Japanese pastors took on the tasks of running the churches in town, which included performing services and attending to all the other details. However, we were pelted with stones

---

[37] Somen is a kind of noodle. Trans.

and subjected to other types of harassment. At those times I recalled the words that John Wesley had been told by his father: "Even though you are persecuted, you must not retaliate. You must not fight back."

One time at school, when the teacher was absent, we had some free time. We boys liked to play a game called "play fighting" where we would wrestle. Everyone thought I was weak and pounced on me. I was stronger than they expected, though, and let them have it, one after the other. My friends said, "You usually never fight back when you are bullied, so how come you can defend yourself so well?" When I told them that I practiced kenjutsu, their attitude toward me changed and I was treated like a hero. It was an episode in which martial arts really saved me.

After the war ended, I entered middle school at the Tō-ōgijuku. Even though I still attended church, I didn't have to care about what others thought about it. At the time, there were many unbelievably poor and physically and mentally disadvantaged people around. They formed into communities – outcasts, people called *baka* in the Tsugaru dialect, and children abandoned by their parents because they had physical disabilities. They made their homes under bridges and barely managed to survive.

The parishioners of our Church brought them food, and I became friends with one of the children from the group called *baka*. I think he was a few years older than me. One day the sunset was very beautiful. My friend pointed at the sky and said, "God is in the clouds of this sunset. I can see angels." His words shocked me. I thought I was pious, and I wasn't slow, but did not see God in the sky, nor did I see angels swathed in the clouds. This encounter opened my eyes and helped me understand that the people from these communities were humble and unpretentious. This planted the seed in my mind that to be unassuming and down-to-earth like my friend, I needed to become a minister.

Figure 12: The Katayama Cabinet. Junzo is second from the right.

In 1946, my father ran for the Diet in the first post-war election and took the top number of votes to become a member of the House of Representatives from Aomori. This was what the graduates of the Tō-ōgijuku had hoped for. The next year he became a Minister of State in the Katayama Cabinet where he held posts as the Director General of the Repatriation Agency and the President of the Demobilization Board. Our family once again returned to Tokyo.

The Nightmare That Was the Prohibition of Kendo

Together with Okada Seiichi, my father formed a political party called the People's Party. This party merged with Miki Takeo's Cooperative Democratic Party to form the People's Cooperative Party. Shortly thereafter, the People's Democratic Party was born, and then the Japan Progressive Party merged with Hatoyama Ichiro and his followers to become the Japan Democratic Party. This later evolved into the Liberal Democratic Party.

While my father crossed swords with the military authorities of Imperial Japan during the war, he ended up fighting with military authorities once again in General Douglas MacArthur's General Headquarters (GHQ) after the war ended when he objected to their efforts to prohibit the practice of kendo and naginata. The American military remembered very well how, during combat, Japanese soldiers attacked with a strong spirit, and they concluded that the practice of kendo and naginata were at the heart of militarism in Japan. They disestablished the All-Japan Butokukai, which promoted and provided education about various types of martial arts and was sponsored by the Imperial Family. Also, though kendo had been a compulsory subject in middle schools since 1931 under the Imperial education system, the GHQ prohibited it from being taught in all public schools.

Neither kendo nor naginata had ever countenanced uncivilized forms of behavior. My father, who would not accept this destruction of traditional Japanese culture, attempted to persuade GHQ to lift the ban and finally succeeded after two or three years of trying. The San Francisco Peace Treaty came into force in 1952 and put an end to the U.S. occupation of Japan. Before the occupation ended, however, he was suspected of being a militarist due to his ties to kendo and was apparently targeted for expulsion from public office by the Americans.

Due to his connections to GHQ, he was involved in another meeting with the same Baker and companion who had met Foreign Minister Matsuoka before the war. General MacArthur invited them both to Japan to review the condition of the Japanese education system. As before, Baker met with the Emperor. During their pre-war visit, my father had loaned them dress coats so they would be properly attired for the meeting. When Baker explained this to the Emperor during his post-war visit, I heard that Emperor Hirohito replied, "Is that what happened? From now on, please use the Christian lesson of love to promote world peace."

After the war, we moved to a detached house in the Den-en-Chōfu area of Tokyo. It was a nice area, and we were fortunate that Ishizaka Yōjirō, a native of Hirosaki and author of the novel, *Aoi sanmyaku*, lived near us. At the time it was normal for politicians to have no money, but if a parliamentarian accepted an official position in a political party he would have to pay the party for it, so we had to sell the house. After the singer Akatsuki Teruko bought the house from us, we moved to the Komaba area in the Meguro Ward of Tokyo.

What my father tried to do as a politician was to have politics discussed in the Diet. Even when the Diet was in session, debate there often stopped for a variety of reasons, such as parliamentarians being investigated for corruption or due to power struggles between parties. Instead, so-called political heavy hitters would meet at high class restaurants and decide important matters in back-room deals. There were also various political reporters hanging

Figure 13: Father and son demonstrating Ittō-ryū in Osaka.

around and my father absolutely refused to provide them with favors so they would write positive stories about him. This led them to say things like, "He is cheap and close-minded." However, I still have vivid memories of him working extremely hard.

I advanced to Aoyama Gakuin Middle School and continued to attend church. At school, I joined the Young Men's Christian Association and decided that I would be baptized after I graduated. In the Catholic tradition, baptism is done when children are still infants, but in the Protestant traditions it is left up to the individual to decide when to be baptized. In some denominations, one may be baptized as a child, but in the more traditional ones a person cannot be baptized until they become an adult and are able to express their faith by their own volition.

Around this time, I also started to practice Ono-ha Ittō-ryū in earnest. I became my father's training partner after I entered Aoyama Gakuin High School, and we started to increase the amount of practice we did. Our family dojo had yet to be built at that time, so we had to practice in the yard around our house. I remember that when my father would pull out a thirty-three inch sword with a blunted edge called a *habiki* that we used for training it would shock people walking by. From a short distance away it looked like we were using real swords.

My father even taught Ono-ha Ittō-ryū to various instructors of modern kendo. They learned by first watching my father and me demonstrate techniques and then practicing themselves. My father often admonished me, "If your opponent scores a point on you, you should not think, 'Damn you!' or 'Darn it.' You were hit because you had an opening in your defense. Your opponent was teaching you where your weak points are, so you should say, 'Thank you.' If you cannot say that, then you cannot say you are doing true kendo."

Still pursuing my dream of becoming a minister, I planned to enter the Aoyama Gakuin University Department of Theology and study Christianity. But my father, who normally never said anything about my path in life, raised a rare objection: "If you want to be a minister, you should learn about the world. You should study somewhere else to do that." Heeding this advice, I entered the Waseda University School of Literature, Department of Philosophy.

"Joe" Whom I Met at the Tō-ōgijuku

After graduating from Waseda without any problem and wondering how I was going to find a job, I happened to learn that the Tō-ōgijuku was looking for a teacher. This school had been reorganized in 1947 along post-war educational guidelines, and a middle school was established as part of that reorganization. With a recommendation from my father, I was hired as soon as I applied. At first I taught Japanese language, but the teacher in charge of the sophomore class in high school suddenly fell ill and retired, and I, a newly minted teacher, was hastily transferred in to replace him. This was an experience I never forgot when I became a minister.

There were students in my new class who could be unruly, even in the middle of their lessons. The highly capable student leader approached me and complained when this happened. "Teacher, why don't you yell at them when they act up in class?" I replied, "I will never scold them. If they hear me yelling at them in anger, it will be like yelling at a dog or a cat. They are human beings, so if I don't raise my voice and they still don't quiet down, won't they feel embarrassed?"

I thought about finding a good way to keep them quiet, though, and one day, while standing on the teacher's platform, I pulled out a thirty-three inch sword I had brought with me when I transferred from Tokyo and showed it to them. I also showed them a technique to knock over an opponent without touching them just by projecting internal energy (kiai 気合). This was something I had learned from Mr. Fujita Seiko, the sōke of the Kōga-ryū school of ninjutsu. He was an acquaintance of my father and often came to visit our home. After seeing this demonstration, the students quieted down and the complaints from the student leader stopped.

In the class there was one student, I will call him "Joe," who was a year older than the others. He suffered from an addiction to Philopon. Philopon is an amphetamine that was commonly sold over the counter before the war. It had been banned five years previously, in 1951, when the Stimulants Control Act was passed, but it was still not unusual to encounter people addicted to it. His previous teacher was a very generous man. Even though he was just married, he put up Joe in his house and generally looked out for him. He fell ill and left and Joe must have felt very alone after that.

At the Tō-ōgijuku, teachers took turns staying at the school overnight, patrolling the campus. When it was my turn to pull duty, Joe started to tag along. We played chess, ate, and made the rounds in the middle of the night together. One time he muttered, "Normal teachers get mad, but you don't. When I look in your eyes I get scared. I wonder what you are thinking." He had been tagging along to secretly find out more about me. I started to look after him, as his previous teacher had done, and he accompanied me when I patrolled the school. We started to become close friends.

One time he grew his hair out. At the time, it was the norm for high school students to keep their hair in a crew-cut. Only third-year students were allowed to grow their hair out so they could start their post-graduation job hunt. Joe was still a second-year student, though, and the length of his hair became a problem at a faculty meeting. As I was the person in charge of his educational development, my fellow teachers confronted me and told me to warn him about keeping his hair short.

When I advised Joe to cut his hair, he retorted, "But the third-year students are allowed to grow their hair out!" I said, "Well, they are looking for jobs," but he wouldn't listen, arguing, "I might look for a job, too." Being as green as I was, I reported to my colleagues at our next faculty meeting that Joe said he did not want to cut his hair. They just got mad and said, "Why are you being so soft on him? Make him cut his hair!"

When I next spoke to Joe, I said, "The other teachers are angry, so how about getting a haircut?" but he refused to listen and instead cut his hair into a Mohawk in complete defiance. "This haircut is what I think of the school and the teachers!" he said. This created even more tension, with my fellow teachers calling for him to be suspended or expelled. I was between a rock and a hard place, having just asked Joe to cut his hair.

I don't know if I should consider this a stroke of good luck, but I was hit with appendicitis and hospitalized. The first person to visit me was Joe. He came into the room carrying a bottle of grape juice, which he knew I liked, and said, "I came to visit." I was surprised to see that he had cut his hair, but I did not say anything about it and neither did he. He went home after he was done visiting.

That year, we celebrated Christmas. Every year, the chapel of the Tō-ōgijuku was opened to the public and hosted a Christmas party that included members of the community who lived near the school. Joe told me he wanted to go, so we decided to go together. As a teacher, I normally would sit in the front, but this time I sat in the back with Joe. All of a sudden he said, "I want to be baptized," and all I said was, "That sounds good!" In April of the following year he became a Christian.

Some Things Only a Minister Can Do

I resigned and returned to Tokyo after only one year as a teacher at the Tō-ōgijuku. This was because I finally made up my mind to become a minister. Thanks to my experience with Joe, I came to firmly believe that getting mad at students and punishing them served no purpose. To help children in the world who are troubled, you first have to accept that they have sinned and then forgive them. My time with Joe made me realize that granting forgiveness in the true sense of the word is something I could do only as a minister.

Shortly thereafter, I wrote a letter to my father in Tokyo and informed him that I had considered various options and settled on becoming a minister. I was happy to learn that, though he had shown a circumspect attitude toward me pursuing that path, wondering if I had had enough life experience, he approved.

I entered Aoyama Gakuin Christian Studies Department as a graduate student and, after two years of study at the seminary, earned my credentials as a minister. In 1959, I submitted an application to work as the minister of the church within the Aoyama Gakuin, but my father once again offered some advice: "If you are going to serve as a minister, you should do it right by studying at a seminary in America." That summer I decided to leave for the United States.

"For theology, study in Germany; to learn how to run a church, study in America."—This was what I was told by a wide variety of people connected with Christianity. They recommended America rather than Europe because many brilliant theologians had escaped from Germany and found asylum in the United States during World War II. Also, as I have written previously, America was founded by the Puritans, a Protestant faction that had broken away from the Church of England. You could say that from the perspective of how Christianity was taught and how it was applied to people's daily lives, America was a better place to learn than the countries of Europe. Still, it was a time when I set out for a foreign country with no more than twenty-five dollars in my pocket. It was truly a rough educational experience.

At first, I entered the Seminary of Duke University in the state of North Carolina. It took me three years to do a two-year master's course and I finished in 1961. I took advantage of this opportunity to marry my wife, to whom I proposed before I left for overseas study. We met when she was studying theology at Aoyama Gakuin. Thanks to the kindness of some friends, we were able to have our marriage ceremony in the Duke University Chapel.

While I was studying abroad, there were times when the martial arts I learned from my father came in handy. One time, an American football player stirred up some trouble by saying, "Judo from Japan is no big deal. I took on a Japanese student who was a black belt (3rd degree) and when I laid on top of him, I crushed him." I decided to take him on.

He came forward to crush me like he did to the judoka. I used *taijutsu* techniques from Ono-ha Ittō-ryū (taijutsu skills are unarmed combat techniques, similar to jujitsu, which was the origin of Judo). Ono-ha Ittō-ryū is a school of kenjutsu, but many of the old fencing schools of Japan also taught how to fight empty handed. Instantly, I turned the tables on a guy who seemed to be about twice my size. "That was amazing!" he exclaimed, and he asked me to demonstrate some of these skills at his hometown high school. After that, he restored the reputation and honor of

Japanese martial arts by giving me a tour of his town in a convertible.

After I graduated from the seminary, I lived in New York for a while and then moved to Connecticut. During the week, I attended a seminary in Hartford and on the weekends traveled to New York City to work as a minister in a church catering to Japanese-speaking parishioners.

Around this time I met an American missionary I had known from before. He was one of the missionaries who had done mission work in Tokyo before the war and returned home after being ordered to leave by the Foreign Ministry. He explained that he had been imprisoned in the United States as a conscientious objector after refusing to serve in the military. While in prison, an Army officer visited him saying, "We are going to bomb Tokyo and I would like to discuss where we should target and what we should avoid." He explained that Meiji Gakuin had continued to provide Christian education and had not closed down but wasn't sure about Aoyama Gakuin. In fact, Aoyama Gakuin was bombed and over half of the school burned to the ground. I received this information first-hand.

My father stopped by New York on his way to attend an international conference in South America while he was serving as the Chair of the Foreign Affairs Subcommittee for the House of Representatives. When he visited, he said he intended to turn our home into both a dojo and a church, and wanted to know if I could return home soon. It was my father's long-cherished dream to create a place that would serve both as a dojo where we could practice Ittō-ryū and a church where we could observe our Christian faith. Since he did not have enough funds to build the church, he asked me to raise the money in New York.

I threw myself into the task, expecting to return to Japan soon, when I came across my dream job. I was offered a position as the director of a newly established Japanese language department in one of the universities in New York. At the same time, the parishioners of the Japanese church in New York, who were surprised to hear about my intention to return home, offered to double my salary to get me to stay. *Should I go home? Should I stay?* Something happened one day while I was trying to decide.

The Sign: *What are You Doing?*

After I completed my services in New York one Sunday, I stayed late to work and ended up spending the night there. I got up early the next morning and started the eighty-mile drive to our home in Hartford, speeding along the expressway with my wife in the passenger seat. The highway had steep drop-offs on both sides and a median divider that also formed a cliff. Suddenly, the car skidded. I tried to correct the skid somehow and braked to keep from sliding off either side of the road, but the car spun out. We eventually came to a stop pointing in the opposite direction, facing on-coming traffic.

Just as I got out of my car to direct the cars coming toward us, I saw that another person was already standing there stopping traffic. A highway patrolman showed up shortly thereafter. After the policeman stopped his car along the shoulder of the road, he stepped over the guardrail and motioned for me to move my car out of the way.

Water had collected in potholes in the road and then frozen, and when one of my tires hit one of these patches of ice, the car had started to skid. It was not a major accident, but I held up traffic behind me. When the policeman saw we were unhurt, he allowed us to continue on our way. But when I looked for the man who had stopped traffic for me to thank him, he was gone. He may have gotten back into his car and left before I noticed. However, I never saw him completely, or even the car he was driving. Looking back on it, when I got out of my car right after we spun out, all I ever saw was the upper half of his body. *Was it really a person?* I wonder... In due course I realized that something saved my life, and this incident made me stop and think: *what am I really doing?*

I could no longer stay in America due to my visa status and the money situation. I viewed this accident as a sign that I had to make a change. I had originally gone to America so I could be better prepared to spread the Gospel in Japan, so I viewed this experience as a call to return home.

I made up my mind and returned to Japan in 1969 when I was thirty-six years old. Ten years had passed in America by the time I resumed my life in Japan. When I returned, my home had already been rebuilt, with our family residence on the first floor and the church-*cum*-dojo on the second. My father named the dojo Reigakudo. The official opening of the dojo had been done in a Christian-style ceremony.

When I went inside to look around, I saw that some items that I had sent ahead were placed on the altar that was handmade by my father. There were a cross and sconces donated by the volunteers from my old church in

New York as well as a baptism and collection bowl donated by my roommate from Duke University.

The only thing left to decide was what to call the church. At first, my father and I considered naming it the Sasamori Memorial Church but thought it was too much associated with our family name. We then thought of calling it the Misakae no Den (御栄の殿).[38] This can be contracted to Eden (栄殿), as in the Garden of Eden from which Adam and Eve were expelled when they refused to repent their sins and which is guarded by an angel who wields a flaming sword.[39] The story of the angel driving Adam and Eve from the Garden of Eden is also reminiscent of the sword in Ittō-ryū called the *manjiken*, which can be likened to the sword wielded by the cherubim. By combining these two ideas, we decided to christen it as the Komaba Eden Church.[40]

Since I had already been ordained, I became the first generation minister of the church. The process of becoming ordained is similar to how a medical doctor earns a national medical license. Merely passing a test is not enough, and one must serve as an intern and work at a church as an assistant pastor as part of the ordination process. After passing yet another exam, one can serve as a fully qualified minister. This type of certification process has been preserved by the United Church of Christ in Japan (headquartered in Tokyo's Shinjuku Ward).

---

[38] Translated as *Palace of the Lord*. Trans.

[39] This refers to the flaming sword wielded by the cherubim, the angel that guards the Garden of Eden: "He drove out the man; and at the east of the Garden of Eden he placed the cherubim, and a flaming sword which turned every way, to guard the way to the tree of life." Genesis 3:24 (RSV). Trans.

[40] *Komaba* is a place name in Tokyo. Trans.

Within the newly constructed building that housed the Komaba Eden Church, both the church and the kenjutsu dojo were, essentially, one and the same. This was my father's long-cherished wish.

The Birth of the Komaba Eden Church

Once I settled into my new life back in Tokyo, I was shocked when I noticed the deplorable condition of Japan's youth. The year before, Japan had climbed to having the second largest economy in the world as measured by GNP. It was probably due to Japan becoming a wealthy nation, but the middle and high school students I encountered were indifferent to social problems and would not engage in conversations about serious issues going on around them. They only thought about getting rich, having sex, and falling in love. At the time, it was all about having fun. I was troubled by this and felt I had to do something.

This was my major motivation for once again standing in front of students at the Aoyama Gakuin Middle School. While I was in America, the school had asked me to return as a minister to teach there. The first time I declined, but when I paid a visit to the school after returning to Japan, the administration said, "We have not yet decided on a teacher who will teach the Bible to our middle school students as an in-residence minister. We really want you to join us." Since they waited such a long time for me to return, I accepted their offer and started working as a minister assigned to the Aoyama Gakuin Middle School.

Not long after, in February of 1976, my father passed away.

As I discussed previously, during his ninety years with us he took on various responsibilities stemming from his deep mastery of both paths of Christianity and kenjutsu. As an educator in the post-war era, he served as the President of the Japan Economic Junior College and was also involved in establishing the International Christian University. As a politician, while serving more than twenty years in the House of Representatives, he worked toward instilling a sense of ethics in politics and government as a Minister of Home Affairs, receiving the Grand Cordon, Third Class. He also became the sōke of the Ono-ha Ittō-ryū and Shinmusō Hayashizaki-ryū schools of kenjutsu, the sōke of the Chokugen-ryū school of naginata, and served both as the first Chairman of the All-Japan Student Kendo Federation and as a Supreme Advisor to the All-Japan Kendo Federation.

While he was on the world stage performing these duties he was often stabbed in the back. He had an abiding faith in his fellow martial artists, and would say, "There are no bad people among those who practice the Way of the Sword." But when they would really deceive him and I would say, "But surely there are bad people, even among sword experts," he would reply, "Those people don't know the true meaning of the Way of the Sword." Also, despite his many achievements, he lived such a humble and simple life that it surprised all who came in contact with him.

He often used to say, "Slow but steady," in English. I can only guess why he said this just in English, but I suppose it was because it was difficult to translate the nuances of this phrase into Japanese and he liked the sound of it. He also used to say, "I am proud of you. You are my proud [sic]." These are words that I still treasure.

After my father passed away, we wrestled with what to do about the Komaba Eden Church. Because my eldest brother had died while an infant and my second eldest brother had become a musician, it was only natural for me to succeed my father, not only as the head of the church but also as the sōke of Ono-ha Ittō-ryū, Shin Muso Hayashizaki-ryū, and Chokugen-ryū.

There were missionaries who worked hard to spread Christianity in Japan after the Meiji Restoration. There were sword experts who taught Ono-ha Ittō-ryū. There were Uchimura Kanzō and Nitobe Inazo, as well as young men from samurai families, who pursued both paths in their own way. I am certainly not as accomplished as them but want to follow the same paths they did nonetheless.

In the Bible, it is written that when God created Heaven and Earth he surveyed all he created and was pleased. But the wonders that he created were not limited to the purview of Western civilization. He was also pleased with what he created in Japan. It is because he created something good in Japan that I want to offer my thanks to him, and I think it would be good if we were able to use what he bestowed upon Japan to serve him.

What is this good thing that he created in Japan? This may sound self-serving, but I believe it is the Japanese spirit epitomized by Bushido. Uchimura believed that Christianity should be grafted onto the trunk of the tree called Bushido. Even if it is not grafted onto Bushido, however, I am still grateful to God for giving us Bushido, which is the quintessence of Japanese culture and which we Japanese can offer for the betterment of mankind. My conception and principle purpose in life has not been to graft Christianity onto Bushido but to find connections between Christianity and both Bushido and Japan itself.

How do you find these connections? You start by not having preconceived ideas about these Ways, but examining them directly and then getting to know them in your heart and soul.

Chapter 6

Does Christianity Accept Ritual Suicide; Is There Love in Bushido?

Three Reasons There Are Not More Christians in Japan

If Christianity and Bushido have never been incompatible, and if, to the contrary, it was only natural that those who deeply studied one of these Ways would come to understand the other, then why didn't the number of Christians dramatically increase after the ban on Christianity was lifted in Japan? I would like to address this very pointed question below. In this chapter, I want to start by bringing the similarities between these two Ways into focus by comparing key aspects of both.

There are three major reasons why the spread of Christianity faced difficulties in Japan. The first is that when it was first introduced, Japanese people had extremely limited opportunities to be exposed to it. This may be a generalization, but with every generation the number of warriors who diligently studied the martial arts and who truly understood Bushido became fewer and fewer until, by the of the Edo era, they composed less than ten percent of the population. I wonder who among this ten percent actually came into contact with missionaries and were able to obtain a Bible? Uchimura and Nitobe were very rare examples; commoners did not come close to having the opportunities these two did.

The second reason Christianity did not spread in Japan was how it came to be introduced into this country. The Christians who came to Japan during the Meiji era were predominantly Protestants. These "hired foreigners," who were invited to introduce advanced Western technology and the educational system to Japan, came from England, America, Germany, Holland, and France, which were all, with the exception of France, Protestant nations. Also, many of the missionaries who arrived in Japan were Puritans, a Protestant faction. The Puritans are like the Methodist denomination that I belong to, but even stricter. These days they are not as stringent as in the past, but in the Meiji era they had strictures against drinking, smoking, gambling, and visiting red-light districts. These were all good rules for living a clean life.

Among a warrior class that was used to a life of self-discipline and self-reflection, there was likely little resistance to adapting to this lifestyle, but to the average commoner, Christianity must have appeared unreasonably strict. At the time, it was not unusual for the wealthy or members of high society to have mistresses, but if they were to become Christians, they would have had to put an end to this custom once and for all. I believe many of them kept Christianity at arm's length to avoid having to give up this practice.

Even among the warrior class, there were those who distanced themselves from this faith once they converted. According to Uchimura, this was not because Christianity was bad but because those who did this were weak willed:

> This is not the disgrace of Christianity, it is the shame of all of those who betrayed it, as well as the shame of the Japanese people. Easily throwing

away that which one once believed in, and not being able to respond to the moral demands imposed by Christianity, I have to say is the complete shame of the people.[41]

I would offer that the third reason is that the ban on Christianity imposed by Tokugawa Hidetada continued to exert an influence on society even after it was lifted. In 1549, Francis Xavier of the Jesuit Order of the Catholic Church was the first missionary active in Japan. The Jesuit priests who followed set their sights on the aristocratic daimyo rather than commoners. In the feudal system in Europe, subjects had to follow the faith of their ruling nobility. For example, when the kings of some countries converted to Protestantism, those under their rule also had to convert. To these missionaries, the feudal system in Japan appeared to be the same as the one in Europe, so they approached the nobility in Japan with the idea of converting them, reasoning that once the daimyo converted their subjects would soon follow. These missionaries even offered to help the daimyo procure weapons and ammunition, as well as trade rights with Europeans, in order to obtain permission to proselytize within their domains.

Some of the daimyo who were approached by the Jesuits decided to become Christians on their own volition. Konishi Yukinaga, Kuroda Yoshitaka, and Ōtomo Sōrin of the Bungo Domain (present day Oita Prefecture) as well as Takayama Ukon, who served both Toyotomi Hideyoshi and Maeda Toshiie, came to be known as "Christian Daimyos." While there were, no doubt, daimyo who converted solely to obtain trade rights, Takayama Ukon

---

[41] Uchimura Kanzo, *Diary of a Convert*, Book 15.

and Ōtomo Sōrin became devout believers in Christianity. In fact, there is now an effort underway within Japan to review Takayama's historical legacy and to petition the Vatican to elevate him to sainthood.

When Catholicism began to spread among the common people, however, government officials started to view it as a threat. Consequently, Tokugawa Hidetada issued a decree banning Christianity in the areas under his direct control in 1612, and then expanded the decree the following year to cover the rest of Japan. Persecution started after that, and those found to be Christian were tortured and exiled or killed. As I noted previously, this ban was lifted in 1873. Because it spanned 260 years, it is no surprise that feelings of prejudice and fear of associating with Christians did not immediately disappear amongst the common people after it was lifted, and though the ban on Christianity was, technically speaking, gone, a hang-over effect was that the right to proselytize within Japan was not actually recognized.

In summary, one reason that Christianity did not spread throughout Japan is that there were only a few samurai who acted as a bridge between Japanese society and the Christian faith. The second is that people viewed the Protestant lifestyle as being overly strict. The third is that widespread discrimination against Christianity persisted even after the edicts banning its practice had been lifted. One point I would like to note, though, is that the Japanese people did not reject the teachings of Christianity itself.

Was Steve Jobs Being Zen-Like?

Steve Jobs, the founder of Apple, died in October 2011. Among the many episodes in his life, one of the more famous was a speech he made to the students of Stanford University at a commencement ceremony. In this speech he said, "Remembering that you are going to die is the best way I know to avoid the trap of thinking you have something to lose."

Because Jobs was known in Japan to be a devotee of Zen, I think these words were interpreted as evidence of how close his personal philosophy was to Bushido. However, despite his devotion to Zen, I wonder if he was also greatly influenced by Christian philosophy. This is because I can find eschatological passages in the Bible that convey a similar sense of resignation that *someday the end will come.*

So, from here on, I would like to compare lessons in both Bushido and Christianity by first discussing death and love. You could say that, as humans, we have both strong moral values and a daily reality we have to face. Is Christianity incompatible with the code of Bushido that encourages death? Also, Christianity preaches love, but can you find the concept of love in Bushido?

The saying, "The way of Bushido is to seek death," from the book *Hagakure* is often cited as the passage that best describes the essence of Bushido. But the meaning of this is often misunderstood because it was used by Imperial Japanese military officers during World War II to justify sending soldiers and sailors to their deaths on kamikaze missions and suicide attacks. The fact is, however, that this maxim does not encourage you to throw your life away needlessly, as in "you can kill yourself for any reason." It means that you should not be frightened of dying if it is for the sake of your personal beliefs, faith, values, or a just cause. The spirit of this passage conveys that you should live your life fully, doing your best every day, so that no matter when you die you can do so without regret or shame. By living your life this way, death leads to life and life leads to death. The type of death that I am talking about here is not an abstract concept but a concrete and specific image of a situation in which someone could die at any moment, such as when they get into an accident or face some other life-or-death situation. The samurai sought true meaning in death. Death challenged them to ask themselves if they could sacrifice everything for what they personally believed in.

Other passages of the *Hagakure*, in contrast, state that surviving is also part of the Way of the Warrior. It took courage for them to escape when they were surrounded by their enemies, and this, as well, was not at all inconsistent with the code of Bushido. In other words, to the samurai who followed the Bushido code, it was always important to clearly understand what they were living for and what they should die for. Said another way, it means that they would have gladly died for something worth protecting.

We do not know if our time to die will be today or tomorrow. However, if we always think we are going to die, the best way to live our lives today will come to us. In the next section, I will consider more closely the idea of death being life.

Die First, Then Defeat Your Enemy

The *Hagakure* contains a description of how Nitta Yoshisada, a general who lived during the end of the Kamakura period, met his end. Nitta managed to cut off his own head and bury it, and then lay on top of the dirt mound and died. They say that *how* he died is what astonished his enemies and frightened them away. Regardless of whether this actually happened, it is important to note that the point of the story of how he drove away his enemies by killing himself spread far and wide throughout Japan.

Yamamoto Tsunetomo wrote in the *Hagakure* that you should be able to take one more action of consequence even after your head has been cut off. He further elaborated: "A truly brave person is one who can go forward without saying a word and meet their own death. They will not need to kill their opponent. A person who can go to his own death without uttering a word is truly strong. A person like that would be able to defeat any enemy." This idea is also in Christianity. In fact, the story of Saint Denis is just like the anecdote about Nitta Yoshisada.

Relief sculptures of human figures adorn the facade of a church in the northern part of Paris, France that is described as a masterpiece of Gothic construction. Among the figures carved into the façade, there is one that is watched over by two angels but is headless. This figure carries his own head in his hands. This is the third century missionary Denis.

As legend has it, Denis arrived in Paris before Christianity had taken root there and lived under the patronage of the local pagan king. The king's closest advisors became jealous, however, and had him arrested and sentenced to death for worshiping Jesus as the supreme God, rather than the king. The king offered to pardon him, but Denis refused to worship the king over God. Eventually, he was summoned to the executioner's hill and beheaded.

After the execution, Denis managed to pick up his own head and carry it downhill toward the center of Paris. It is no surprise that, after watching this spectacle from beginning to end, the king and all of the astonished onlookers converted to Christianity. The hill where he was executed is now called *Montmarte* (Martyr's Hill), and a chapel has been constructed on the spot where he was executed. They have both become famous tourist attractions.

The point of bringing up the anecdotes about both Nitta Yoshisada and Saint Denis is merely to convey the idea that one can defeat an enemy through his own death. Death is not dying but life, living, and making the best use of one's life. These old tales are hard to believe, but I wonder if there are hidden truths in these legends that have withstood the test of time.

Is there a Difference between the Ritual Suicide of Harakiri and Following One's Lord in Death?

There are probably people like the missionaries I introduced in the foreword of this book who will say that Bushido is incompatible with Christianity because it is a philosophy that calls for ritual suicide and advocates vengeance.[42] But I would like you to consider the

---

[42] Ritual suicide as discussed in this chapter is known as both *harakiri* (腹切) and *seppuku* (切腹). Both terms mean the same thing and refer to the ritualistic cutting of the stomach region. It was not uncommon for vassals to commit suicide in this manner upon the death of their lords as a show of fealty. This practice, known as *junshi* (殉死), was outlawed in Japan by various governments over the centuries but continued into the twentieth

following questions. The first is whether the ritual suicide described in Bushido is really suicide. Suicide is the act of killing oneself due to an inability to deal with life's hardships or due to intense suffering caused by mental illness or other factors. You could say that one definition of suicide is that it is giving up on the responsibility to keep living.

The ritual suicide that was part of the code of Bushido, however, is not at all about abandoning responsibility; to the contrary, it was about accepting responsibility. It did not entail samurai killing themselves secretly, out of the view of others, but was done in public and in accordance with strict rules of etiquette. People today may wonder if it was necessary to go to such extremes. After all, in the modern world the chairman of the board of a private company typically takes responsibility for some misdeed by resigning his post, and parliamentarians merely remove their lapel pins when they resign from the National Diet. To the samurai, however, accepting death showed how seriously they took their duties, and ritual suicide became the ultimate expression of this.

Also, by meeting their fate through the act of *harakiri*, they ensured their names would live on forever. Their name was their soul, and having their name live on forever meant that they would exist for eternity. The act of committing ritual suicide enabled them to further this existence with their dignity intact. Going to such an extreme may seem like an act of fanaticism by today's standards, but to the samurai, the idea of shame was

---

century. The most recent example was that of General Nogi Maresuke, the hero of the Russo-Japanese War, and his wife, who both committed suicide in 1912 after the death of Emperor Meiji. Trans.

vitally important. Not accepting responsibility for their own actions brought disgrace, and they chose the honor of death over living a life of shame.

Flowers Blossom After You Die

On the other hand, suicide is prohibited in Christian doctrine because Christianity teaches that one must not take the life that God has given them. You could say that there are two very important times in a person's life which they are never able to decide for themselves: birth and death. People cannot choose when or under what circumstances they will be born or die. This is because Christians believe that these two events are determined by God, and there is an outright prohibition against taking one's own life that one must never disobey.

What I would like you to consider, however, is that the history of Christianity is closely associated with the history of martyrs, and Christians do not view the actions of these martyrs as violating their faith. When persecuted by another, a person's normal reaction would be to pick up a weapon and fight back, but Christians never fought back at all against those persecuting them. The times they were arrested and sent to exile, they never tried to escape.

Another way of viewing this is that they went to meet their own deaths. This is because they were likely to be sentenced to death once they were arrested. For example, during the Roman era, after Christians were tortured they were thrown into dungeons. Then they were called out, one by one, and executed. The faithful in the prisons prayed and sang hymns while quietly waiting for the day they would be killed. There is absolutely no evidence to suggest that they resisted or engaged in activities like fomenting rebellions or trying to escape. To the martyrs who were killed, dying was considered to be nothing more than expressing their faith through their own deaths. Churches were built on the very spots where they were executed.

Peter was a loyal disciple of Jesus and also one of the Twelve Apostles painted by Leonardo da Vinci in his work the *Last Supper*. As legend has it, after Jesus' death, Peter took his wife to Rome to preach the Gospel but left the city after facing ever-increasing persecution. While traveling on the road leading away from Rome, Peter met Jesus on the same road walking in the opposition direction. Peter asked, "Lord, where are you going?" and Jesus replied, "Since you have abandoned my people, I am going to Rome to once again be crucified on the cross." Hearing this, Peter turned around and headed back to Rome.

He was arrested when he arrived, and his wife was burned at the stake. Believing that he did not deserve to be crucified like Jesus, he convinced the Romans to crucify him on a cross planted upside down. His dying words were: "If I am to give glory to God, I will die while singing his praise. I am not afraid, for though you can kill my flesh, you cannot kill my soul." As I will explain in the next chapter, because Christians believe that even though their bodies die their souls live on forever, he was expressing his conviction that he would enter another world after death.

There is a Japanese proverb, "Flowers don't blossom after you die," but considering that after they died for the sake of their beliefs their names would live on, the motivations that drove the samurai to the ritual suicides described in the *Hagakure* and the martyrdom described in the Bible are really the same. Furthermore, of all of the martyrs in the Bible, the one whose death was most significant was Jesus.

When Jesus Christ was crucified the crowd verbally mocked him, saying such things as: "If you are really the Savior, let's see you get down off the cross," "You can save others but cannot save yourself?", and "Why don't you call your army of saviors?"

Jesus said, "Father forgive them, for they know not what they say," and after he said, "It is finished," he died.

What would have happened if Jesus had actually come down off of the cross? Many of Jesus' disciples were around him, and it is not impossible to think that they could have fought back the crowds. Had they done so, they could have started a rebellion or even founded a new country, but that would have ended as merely a single episode in the long history of the world. It may have even ended up as a simple entry in a Japanese history textbook. It is precisely *because* Christ died on the cross that we continue to speak of his love after two thousand years, and it continues to save people today.

Jesus said of death: "...Unless a kernel of wheat falls to the ground and dies, it remains only a single seed. But if it dies, it produces many seeds." (John 12:24 RSV) No matter what kind of seed is planted, it transforms in shape, becomes a new sprout, and that sprout becomes a stalk which grows thick with flowers that bear dozens or hundreds of more seeds. In order to do this, the seed first has to die once in the ground. Furthermore, Jesus said, "...Whoever wants to be my disciple must deny themselves and take up their cross and follow me. For whoever wants to save their life will lose it, but whoever loses their life for me will find it." (Mathew 16: 24-25 RSV)

Death does not bring the end but brings about life. The major paradox in the Christian faith is that one must die in order to truly live. It is within this paradox where Christianity and the spiritual milieu that has shaped the Japanese people closely converge.

The Four Types of Love Taught in the Bible

But what about love, which is at the opposite end of the spectrum from death? I will examine this first from the Christian perspective. The Japanese translation of the Bible expresses the general concept of love using only two words, *love* and *affection*, but when you read the Bible in Hebrew and Greek, there are four types of love. All four are reviewed below.

The first type of love is *chesed*, which is described in the Old Testament book of Hosea. The prophet Hosea had been betrayed by his wife, Gomer. Gomer took a lover and abandoned Hosea to live with him. Hosea paid money to get her back again and again. Although she was an unfaithful wife, he continued to love her. This kind of love is called *chesed*. Chesed is love in which one forgives and accepts another even after being betrayed by them over and over again. Translated, chesed implies *having deep affection for* and *unconditional love*.

In fact, this story illustrates the unconditional love that God showed toward the Jewish people. The Jews are God's chosen people, and though he watched over them closely, he was constantly betrayed by them. During the period covered by the Old Testament, pantheistic religions flourished in the lands around Israel. The people of Israel were enamored of these other faiths and worshiped their gods. Despite this, God never abandoned them. This is an example of chesed. Simply put, the love of God toward the Jewish people described above is like the story of Hosea. God is like the husband, while Israel is like the unfaithful wife. This is an example of chesed, the highest form of love.

Why do people betray another's love? It is because humans are inevitably born with sin. This is a bit off topic, but I would like to explain further. The concept of original sin as described in Christianity is rather difficult for many people to understand. There are probably those who question how you could commit a sin immediately after being born, in other words, an original sin, and wonder what kind of sin could one possibly commit.

To give a detailed explanation, the reader has probably heard the story of how Adam and Eve violated a commandment by God and ate fruit from the *Tree of Knowledge of Good and Evil* and were then subsequently banished from the Garden of Eden. There are many, however, who do not understand the significance of this.

I would like you to consider what this means. A snake tempted Eve to eat the fruit by saying, "For God knows that when you eat from it your eyes will be opened, and you will be like God, knowing good and evil." (Genesis 3:5 RSV) Eating this fruit meant that Eve aspired to become a god and, like God, wanted to exist in a state of perfection. But according to Christian doctrine, human beings do not exist in a state of perfection, and no mortal beings are perfect like God. The expulsion of Adam and Eve from the Garden of Eden is not the origin of sin, it is the fundamental nature of sin. Therefore, this is described in English as *original sin* and not *original crime*. Original sin means getting people to acknowledge for themselves that they are not perfect just because they were born.

The German philosopher Karl Jaspers provides an extremely useful analogy. He likened original sin to a flaw in the middle of a crystal. To remove the flaw, you must polish the crystal over and over. The more you polish it, though, the more stone is removed until the entire crystal eventually disappears. What he was saying is that human existence itself would disappear if people were to try to remove original sin. Jasper was teaching that original sin is at the very bottom of people's souls and never goes away.

I find it useful to replace the words *original sin* with *karma* when explaining this to a Japanese audience. Strictly speaking, the concept of original sin has a slightly different connotation than the actions that karma refers to in Buddhism, but when used in the Buddhist context of being beyond redemption (*go ga fukai* 業が深い), which refers to the sinfulness that is at the root of all human beings, this comparison is not too far off.

Returning to *chesed*, one of the four types of love discussed in the Bible, there were figures in the Bible, and people who live today, who constantly conspire to do evil and those who inadvertently get drawn into immoral behavior. The highest form of love that is taught in the Bible, however, is that, no matter what people do, God loves them. Therefore, the Bible teaches that you should believe in God and stay close to him, which is to say, return to his teaching. He will not judge you for what you have done in the past because his real concern is how you live your life from today onward.

Also, when I describe the various forms of love, it conjures up beautiful emotions, but the meaning is more nuanced and includes such elements of interpersonal relations as having trust in, and returning the love of, others. When translating *chesed* from Hebrew into Greek it becomes *agape*. Some may have heard of this word through Greek philosophy.

Who in the World Is My Neighbor?

The remaining three types of love are called *eros*, *philia*, and *storge* in Greek. *Eros* is the taking kind of love that comes from carnal desire. A person desires another for their own pleasure. Sometimes this desire leads a person to kill another who cheats on them. Such a person is not picky about how he gets what he wants. It is the type of love that always continues to take.

Philia is love where one has undying loyalty toward family and friends. In this love, which has a quality that puts it on a level higher than the others, one keeps an abiding faith in their own personal convictions. Lastly, *storge* is love between blood relatives. This is the love associated with personal sacrifice, such as when parents sacrifice themselves for the sake of their children.

Jesus clearly said this about love: "Greater love has no man than this, that a man lay down his life for his friends." (John 15:13 RSV) Of the four types of love discussed above, to which type of love was Jesus referring? Because the phrase *for his friends* is included, one may conclude, at first glance, that this type of love is *philia*, but actually this is the highest form of love, *chesed* (*agape*), the love in which you continue to love someone even after being betrayed by them.

What the word *friends* refers to is *neighbor*. The concept of *neighbor* in Christianity does not literally mean people who live next door to you but all people in the world. In other words, the deepest expression of this love is to sacrifice yourself for the sake of someone else. If a person believes in God and they need to sacrifice themselves for another as a good Christian, they should give their life for them. Jesus taught that you should love others to that extent. When Jesus spoke about loving a neighbor, he did not mean just anyone but really meant you.

Jesus demonstrated this love for his neighbors by being crucified. His crucifixion also meant that everyone should adopt this approach to life. As might be expected, Jesus did not demand that his followers endure the same as he. Just standing idly by when your neighbor is in trouble while saying that you love others or love God, however, is not expressing love either. Jesus taught that if a person is hungry, feed them; if they are naked, clothe them; and if they are in trouble, offer a helping hand. The popularity of social charity programs in the church all come from this basic concept.

Because there is not a single word in Japanese that can convey these four types of love that I introduced, and even in English the simple word *love* is not sufficient either, even English speaking ministers use these categories of love passed on by the Greeks as a means to accurately convey the nuances associated with it.

The Highest Form of Love That the Samurai Never Learned

This brings us to the question of whether love existed in Bushido. You will not find words describing love like those above in the *Hagakure*, but I think they are there in concept. When speaking of love being a part of the Bushido code, you could merely replace it with the words, *fidelity, compassion,* and *sincerity.*

During the Sengoku period, a time when the daimyo increased the size of their domains and income by killing each other, these concepts regarding love were not taught to the samurai. But once Japan entered the Edo period and the metaphysical ideologies of Bushido and Shido started to gain acceptance, warriors started to embrace the concept of love. There were samurai who clearly referred to love in the Bakumatsu period. Saigō Takamori, who was active during the Meiji Restoration, followed the motto "Revere heaven; love people." This phrase meant that one should revere the wrath of heaven and show great affection for others. The samurai who lived at the end of the Edo period knew what it meant to love another person, and we know that they found this important.

The male chauvinism and patriarchy of the Edo period may lead some to think that men domineered over their wives; however, a closer look reveals that samurai both deeply loved and highly valued their families. Even Uchimura Kanzō noted in his writings that women who grew up in samurai households were highly respected and wrote that the notion that women were looked down upon in Bushido was a lie. Also, the episode I described in the first chapter of this book, when Nitobe's mother died and the students of the Sapporo Agricultural College, Uchimura among them, fasted to show their grief, could be described as an example of filial love. I think this shows that the samurai understood very well the types of love in which they were loyal to something they believed in and love that expressed their personal convictions, and that this filial love was on a higher level than the others.

Unfortunately, however, the *chesed* (*agape*) type of love was not considered part of Bushido. *Chesed*, the love shown toward another who continues to betray, was incomprehensible to the samurai who were not Christians. Had the samurai incorporated this type of love into their moral code, such notions as vengeance may have disappeared.

Vengeance was mainly carried out for the honor of the family but also could have been done out of hatred. Even in the popular tale of *Chushingura*, it was because the Forty-Seven Rōnin suffered the indignity of seeing their home domain of Akō seized by the Shogun that they fought a battle on which they staked their personal honor. To the samurai, personal honor came above all else and was much more important than the emotions of love and hate. It was certainly much more important than love.

Just because *chesed* was not part of Bushido, though, does not mean that Bushido is incompatible with Christianity. Bushido is a moral philosophy and a system of ethics, while Christianity is a faith. While there are bound to be differences between them, there are overwhelming similarities when it comes to the concepts of love and death, as we have so far seen, so shouldn't we focus more on what they have in common rather than on their differences?

Jesus Wielded a Double-Edged Sword

Though these two approaches to life may appear similar in theory, there are probably those who wonder if there is a huge contradiction between practicing how to cut an opponent down with a sword by training in the martial arts and remaining true to the path of Christianity. To respond to this question, I will illustrate how the two paths closely resemble each other and how the process of mastering the sword leads to a more pious life by introducing some principles of Ittō-ryū while comparing them with similar lessons in the Bible.

There seems to be a tendency to think that the very existence of a sword goes against the principles of Christianity or that Christianity rejects the sword. This is because of the famous passage in the Bible: "Then Jesus said to him, 'Put your sword back into its place; for all who take the sword will perish by the sword'" (Mathew 26:52 RSV). This is not a rejection of the sword, though. It was an admonition that as long as people believe they should control others through power and violence – using a sword – someone even stronger will come along and use violence against them. What he was saying was that the sword symbolizes the idea of dominating others and that this way of thinking should be abandoned.

We know that Jesus did not reject the sword through the following verse: "Do not think that I have come to bring peace on earth; I have not come to bring peace, but a sword" (Mathew 10:34 RSV). Jesus meant that he came to destroy a society in which the privileged few, like the leaders of Rome and the Pharisees and Sadducees, had control over the masses. The sword is a metaphor and does not imply physically wielding an object; rather, the phrase *bringing a sword* means to prepare to fight against that which is evil and unjust.

The sword traditionally used in Japan has only one edge on the blade, but the sword that was widely used during the time of Jesus was double-edged. Consider for a moment how a sword with two edges cuts as it pierces. When a sword stabs, it not only penetrates but forces apart what it goes into. The following passage is based on this premise: "For the word of God is living and active, sharper than any two-edged sword, piercing to the division of soul and spirit, of joints and marrow, and discerning the thoughts and intentions of the heart" (Hebrews 4:12 RSV).

In fact, this is exactly what Ittō-ryū's secret technique of kiriotoshi does. As I described earlier, when doing kiriotoshi, the opponent's sword is deflected to the side the instant both swords meet and one's own sword cuts into the opponent. We teach that to effectively execute this technique, students must first take stock of their own shortcomings and "cut away" selfish desires, pride, and wickedness. By doing this first, their sword will strike down evil and bring about justice and good.

When kiriotoshi is used to strike down evil in the world, it is called the *Life Giving Sword* (*katsujinken* 活人剣) and the *Sword that is Alive* (*ikutachi* 生く太刀). At the same time, students are admonished that when they take up the sword and face an opponent solely to satisfy their own selfish desires, the sword is referred to as both the *Death Dealing Sword* (*satsujinken* 殺人剣) and the *Sword that is Dead* (*shi ni tachi* 死に太刀).

Moreover, when students execute techniques, one of the things they have to pay close attention to throughout is the concept of *Gokaku Ikkan* (五格一貫), also called *Gokaku Ittei* (五格一締). *Gokaku* refers to the five elements of: mind, *ki*, principle, technical skill and opportunity, which are elements present in every fight. In situations where you face an enemy, you must have the intention, or "mind," to attack. Next, you must extend your ki. When applying your technical skill, it is vital to do so according to proper principles and theories. Then, you must skillfully capitalize on the right opportunity to attack. *Ikkan* (一貫) or *Ittei* (一締) refers to combining these five elements together. No technique can be properly executed if these five elements are not synthesized into a single unit.

A concept similar to this is expressed in Christianity. One cannot be a good Christian by merely feeling or thinking about it. No matter how much they may try, it is not enough to merely perform religious-style meditations, or study theology, or perform public services. Just because someone goes to church once a week does not make them devout either. These are all ways of expressing one's faith, and people should strive to incorporate them all into their daily lives.

What is truly strong is both calm and quiet. In Ittō-ryū, we teach that you should not take an aggressive posture and try to cut down your opponent but stay calm, let him come forward, and respond to what he does. Even if you are extremely skilled, you should not show off but be humble. If you follow these guidelines, it will be only natural for your opponent to back down. To achieve this level of skill, you should apply the overarching principles described above, be self-effacing, and even if you are physically strong, you must become gentle, calm, and peaceful. As I noted in Chapter 3, the objective is to become soft and in harmony with your opponent.

This is similar to what Paul said about Jesus: "Who, though he was in the form of God, did not count equality with God a thing to be grasped, but emptied himself, taking the form of a servant, being born in the likeness of men. And being found in human form he humbled himself and became obedient unto death, even death on a cross. Therefore God has highly exalted him and bestowed on him the name which is above every name" (Philippians 2:6-9 RSV). Sacrificing yourself and becoming empty are concepts that both Bushido and Christianity advocate.[43]

---

[43] The Christian theology of kenosis refers to the self-emptying of one's own will and being receptive to God's divine will. When

Calmly and Skillfully Losing

Stated another way, an expert is really a person who empties themselves and loses quietly and skillfully when it is the right time to lose. An example of an "expert who loses" is described below.

There was a high ranking teacher (ninth dan) of modern kendo who also practiced Zen Buddhism and Ittō-ryū. When this teacher practiced kendo with young students, he would leave his head exposed and let them strike his face mask. When he did this, these youngsters thought, *this teacher is no big deal!* and stepped up their attack. Then he would finally hit them on their face mask. There were students who understood the difference between when he was letting them hit him and when he scored a point on them. They realized he was letting them win. There were also students who never figured this out. This master continued training well into old age and I was saddened by his passing.

He built up his students' confidence, taught them how to win, yet what he was really teaching them was that, in the end, they hadn't beaten anyone. This is the true way to lose. I consider this, in particular, to be the true secret of the martial arts, the original purpose of the martial arts, and even the secret to getting people to put down their swords and stop wars.

It is not difficult to see the common points between kenjutsu and Christianity while practicing Ittō-ryū, and you can come to understand the literal meaning of these

---

one is empty, they are not distracted by extraneous thoughts and, therefore, are receptive to God's will. Kenosis can be compared to the concept of munen-musō, as described earlier. Trans.

lessons through the physical movement of your body when practicing. In my case, this happened after I started practicing the kata of *Goten* (五点), which is another secret of Ittō-ryū on the same level as kiriotoshi. The Goten kata consists of five techniques of: *Myōken, Zetsumyōken, Shinken, Kinshichō Ōken,* and *Dokumyōken* and are learned in that order.

⊖

While Christianity is a religion, Bushido encompasses ethics and perspectives on the life and death of the samurai. It is only natural that there will be a slight difference between them when it comes to the general concept of love, but perhaps the biggest difference between the two is their approach toward matters of the soul.

Bushido is a really wonderful thing but, unfortunately, does not include the concept of salvation. Bushido shows the potential of humans but, at the same time, highlights their limitations. Nobody knows this better than those who practice for a long time. They cannot move faster than is humanly possible, and there is no such thing as physical strength that does not diminish with age. As our physical abilities fade and we eventually die, our corporeal attributes are not carried forward into the next life. Bushido has no answers to the questions regarding the fate that we humans are stuck with, our flaws, and what happens to us after we die.

Chapter 7

Examining the Concept of 'Me' That Is Not Found in Bushido

The Soul: The Personality of 'Me'

These days, it is normal to see Shinto altars in martial arts training halls where judo and kendo are taught. It seems that the custom of putting these altars in these dojos was not practiced in the distant past but only started after State Shinto was established in the Meiji era. Many martial arts masters, however, have looked for common ground between the Japanese martial arts and what is taught in Zen Buddhism and Shinto and sought secrets or pursued salvation and enlightenment from them. Isn't this evidence that, as they got older and realized that the ultimate purpose of martial arts revolved around life and death, they sought answers from the religious world rather than from the code of Bushido? If Christianity had not been banned and had spread throughout Japan, it's possible that many famous sword masters of old, such as Miyamoto Musashi, Tsukahara Bokuden, Ono Jiroemon Tadaaki, and others would have become Christians.

What is not addressed in Bushido, and which it is unable to resolve, is how you should view your soul and what happens to it after you die. Every samurai warrior in the past probably wondered what would happen to him after he passed on. Many were Buddhist, so there were those who thought they would go to heaven or hell, those who thought they would be reincarnated, and also those who thought there was nothing beyond this life.

In contrast, Christians believe that the soul is eternal. Human beings are composed of body and soul, and the soul comes from the spirit. The word *spirit* means the same as *life* and is the power of life bestowed by God. Take, for example, Adam and Eve. God created them out of clay, breathed life into them, gave them a soul, and showed them the way to become living beings. Though the mind may seem to be similar to the soul, it is different and something you can cultivate and develop within yourself. In Christian philosophy, the soul is the power that animates a person while, at the same time, is the root of one's personality of 'me.' The soul – 'me' – is considered to be a blessing from God, so it is very important for people to just be themselves.

As an aside, it is well known that you cannot survive in America if you do not assert yourself. Though in Japan it's very bad to be described as "different," it is not just a word of praise in the United States, but the more Americans behave like the people around them, the more uncomfortable they feel. It is tough to be in a country like that because a child has to assert his or her individuality from a very young age, but in fact, this American way of thinking that "you are one of a kind" is rooted in Christianity. I think the difference between Americans and Japanese is that Americans don't fixate on such questions as, "Am I valuable as a person?" or "Do I have something special others do not?" but just do their best to improve their own individual character.

The Christian Kingdom of Heaven Is Not the Same as the Buddhist Paradise

So what happens to a person's soul after he or she dies? It does not disappear, nor does it change, but returns to God's Kingdom and lives on for an eternity. In other words, 'I' don't change from being 'me.'

It is probably different depending on the faction, but the Buddhist Paradise (*gokuraku* 極楽), generally speaking, is a place where people can get as much food or clothing as they want, where it is neither too hot nor too cold, and where they can live comfortably. The Christian Kingdom of Heaven, however, is completely different from the world in which we currently live.

There is a story in which Jesus himself described what the Kingdom of Heaven was like. In Jewish society in Jesus' time, if the wife of the oldest son was childless and her husband died, she would have to marry one of her husband's brothers. One of the Sadducees who harassed Jesus asked him directly what this law was based upon: "Say that there are seven brothers, and they die one after the other without producing children, and the wife marries all seven. When she is resurrected (and returns to the Kingdom of Heaven), which one is she married to?"

Jesus answered, "The sons of this age marry and are given in marriage; but those who are accounted worthy to attain to that age and to the resurrection from the dead neither marry nor are given in marriage, for they cannot die anymore, because they are equal to angels and are sons of God, being sons of the resurrection." (RSV Luke 20: 34-36) (The same description can be found in Mathew 22 and Mark 12.)

In other words, Jesus was saying that the Kingdom of Heaven has nothing to do with eating or physical health, but that those who reach it lead a completely spiritual existence. This also means that as human beings living on Earth, we only live once–there is no such thing as reincarnation.

This thinking is contrary to the concept of transmigration that is common among Eastern religions such as Buddhism and Hinduism. In these religions, people die and are born again but may or may not be human beings in their next life. What kind of living being they become in the next life depends upon the good or evil deeds they do in their present one.

A friend of mine related some surprising observations about an experience he had while on a trip to India. He encountered a man in a park cheerfully feeding pigeons. Even though a beggar approached close by, the man did not offer him any food. When my friend asked the man why he did not offer the beggar anything, the man replied, "In a past life he did something bad, and now he is in his present condition atoning for his past deeds. This is why I don't need to give him anything." When asked why he prioritized the welfare of the pigeons over another human being, the man replied, "If I don't feed the pigeons, I may become a pigeon in the next life." My friend took away from this a greater appreciation of how reincarnation, rooted in the idea of karmic reward, truly influences how people behave.

Even the caste system in India today, which is currently banned under India's constitution, is underpinned by the idea of transmigration. The caste a person belongs to, whether from the highest caste of Brahmin, to the Shudra, and to those that are lower, is thought to be the result of what that person did in a past life. It seems that this system of social division, however, is not so easy to eradicate.

When I was an exchange student at Duke University, I had a roommate who was a member of the Brahmin caste. He was very diligent in practicing the austerities of his religion, and we both shared the positive experience of living together. One thing I remember well was when he told me that he could talk to his guru in India when he meditated. When I asked him how he was able to do this, he explained that he would call out the holy name of his guru, and his guru would call out the holy name he had given my roommate. By doing so, he reported, the message would go from the Earth to high up in the sky and into space and they would be able to communicate back and forth. As we talked more, I learned that the place the message went to was like the Kingdom of Heaven Christians describe.

In the Hindu faith, after a person dies, his or her soul returns to a sort of chaotic state somewhere, like among the clouds, and at a certain time suddenly descends to Earth where it is reincarnated. If they did good deeds in their previous life, they will become something better. One way of interpreting transmigration is that it contains the notion that a person can control what they become in the next life. This is quite different from the doctrine of Christianity, in which, as I described before, life and death are in God's hands.

So what do Japanese people believe? I wonder if there are not at least as many who believe in transmigration as there are who truly believe that they will go to Heaven or Hell based on what they do in this life. To be frank, I think the answer to this question is summed up in the phrase,

"May his soul rest in peace," which is a common expression used when someone dies.

In Buddhism, *meifuku* is a Japanese word that roughly equates to "rest in peace," and the first half, *mei*, refers to the soul of the deceased going to the world of darkness or the world of the dead. The assumption in Buddhism is that everyone goes there first after they die, so it would be understandable if people were to ask how to get out of such a place, but why is the word *fuku* (good fortune) included in this phrase? Assuming for the sake of argument that the word *mei* simply means *after death*, it seems that Buddhism is trying to imply that this world is a place where no good luck or fortune exists.

The idea that the deeds of this life control what you do or where you end up after you die certainly influences this way of thinking. If people thought that there were two places they could go to after death, they would do their best to do good deeds and behave well in the present world. From a broad perspective, this should lead to a better society and a better country. However, there are downsides to this philosophical approach. I recall a discussion I had with a family that was preyed upon and almost conned out of a substantial sum of money because they believed this.

The Family That Was Tormented by the Fear That Their Grandfather's Soul Was Suffering

When I was still teaching at Aoyama Gakuin, the grandfather of one of my students suddenly died. Judging by the obituaries that came out in the news, he was rather famous. Shortly after the funeral, a stranger visited the home of the grieving family.

"I was just passing by your home and had a strange feeling. Did something happen here?" he asked. When he heard that the head of the house had passed away, he invited himself into their home, saying "Please allow me to pray for him."

In hindsight, this is when the stranger began to swindle the family by using the grandfather's obituary, but at the time this was far from the thoughts of the family and they didn't object. Even so, I think it would be quite difficult for any family to turn down a request from someone who offered to pray on behalf of a loved one.

"Something is wrong," the stranger continued. "Your grandfather is stuck in some other world and worried about moving on to the next. He is suffering. Since I am a member of a kind of religious group that helps departed souls find peace, I will hold a special prayer service to console him. But, you will need to buy prayer beads. This is so his soul can be released to move on to the next world …."

The family purchased the prayer beads. A short time later, the same man returned and reported: "Your grandfather is still in trouble. This situation is beyond my ability to handle." He then recommended that the family visit a facility in the Shinjuku Ward of Tokyo.

When the family went there, they were met by a high-ranking psychic who said, "Your grandfather is suffering very badly. He cannot rest in peace if this situation continues. These prayer beads are not enough. He can be saved, though, if you donate a multi-story pagoda on his behalf."

The five-storied pagoda that the family was asked to buy cost hundreds of thousands of dollars. They didn't have that kind of money, so they refused to pay. When they were about to leave, the psychic approached them again and said, "I just spoke with the soul of your grandfather and he said, 'I don't want to cause trouble to my family members who are still living, so can't you reduce the price for them? My god has said that this is alright, so for a few thousand dollars we can find relief for him." At this point, the family had had enough and visited my church.

After learning about the situation, I advised them that, no matter what kind of person someone is in this life, the idea that his soul suffers after death and that he will be somehow penalized is not right. Moreover, I added, there is no reason to put a family that is mourning the loss of a loved one through that kind of suffering and asked them to forget what the psychics had said. I also offered to speak to the stranger who was conning them. After our conversation, the family's approach toward to their visitor changed, and when the swindlers understood that the family had also consulted a Christian minister, they stopped pestering them. Consequently, the family decided not to purchase the pagoda, but I heard that the grandmother continued to be concerned about the fate of her husband's soul.

I understand this sentiment completely. It is only natural for a person to think that they must do something when they hear that the soul of an ancestor or family member who has died is lost or in trouble. Also, when one is forced to endure an illness or unbelievable suffering, they think there must be some reason for it and that there must be something they can do about it. At times like these, it is very easy for people to think that they are somehow cursed. I can see how people would believe that what they do in this life would somehow follow them into the next, and it is a difficult idea to shake.

On the other hand, this does not mean that the idea that you will face the consequences of your actions in this life after you die is completely absent from the Bible. In Judaism, which is founded on the Old Testament, it is said that after a person who did not follow the laws of God died (the first death), they would face a second death. This second death, also called a spiritual death, is where a person is placed within a darkness called *sheol* where no light or sound can penetrate and where the word of God cannot reach. But this is still not a place of punishment.

When I was young, I had a dream in which I wondered what kind of place this might be, probably after thinking about it too much. Jesus was standing in Heaven while the souls of the departed floated up to meet him and then turned toward a field of flowers. But I also saw that there were souls that were descending into a dark world away from where Jesus was standing. When I asked him why, he replied, "They like it over there." These people chose to live in a location that was only dimly lit after they died and wanted to avoid bright places. I was relieved when I heard this.

Accepting Your Imperfections

Many different kinds of people come to worship at the Komaba Eden Church. In addition to Christian families that regularly attend, students that I taught at Aoyama Gakuin and their parents show up, and sometimes even people who read our sign board outside drop in for a service. A person does not have to convert to Christianity to attend. In fact, many who participate in our regular Sunday sermons are not Christian at all. In the past, only Christians were allowed to attend services, but these days I think there are more churches that open their doors to everyone. Some of these drop-in visitors have even been baptized after becoming more comfortable with the church through such activities as Easter and Christmas services or women's associations.

Christianity is founded on the belief that people do not achieve enlightenment by themselves but live a spiritual life as part of a community. It depends on the church, but in my case, in addition to holding regular sermons, I try to foster close personal relations by sponsoring lunches and other community activities.

As many as one hundred and thirty people attend our Sunday service. I deliver the sermon while wearing a black suit and tie. While ministers in my denomination can wear the cassock and clerical collar like those worn by priests of the Catholic Church, there are many who don't. I wear a dark suit so I don't stand out.

On the very rare occasions that I practice Ittō-ryū after Sunday services, I change into my kenjutsu practice attire. In the past, we wore white training uniforms that we had to keep clean, but these days we wear practice uniforms that are completely indigo-colored and are better for us if we get injured. It may seem like changing clothes causes a change in my behavior or attitude, but that isn't the case at all. I feel that I have both Christianity and Ittō-ryū inside me, and, to me, this is perfectly normal. Those around me, though, to include some parishioners of my church, seem to think something about me changes after I put on my uniform.

In addition to ministering to those who attend my sermons on Sundays, another important part of my job is to counsel those who visit the church to discuss personal matters, such as the family that I previously mentioned. I cannot solve economic problems or heal the sick. There are extremely complex issues associated with these fields of study. Where I try to be helpful is regarding the concern my visitors have about how they deal with their souls, the personality that is 'me.' I would like to provide two examples from my past.

There was a man who suffered for many years from emotional instability. Although he was nearly forty years old, he had never held a steady job and lived off his parents and siblings. To the casual observer he looked normal, but to those closest to him he appeared to be idling away his life. He himself was concerned that if he continued in such a way he would remain a burden on his family. He said that he very much blamed himself for his situation, but when he mentioned this at the hospital the doctors merely increased his medication. I could tell that if his situation didn't change he might very well contemplate taking his own life. Even medical doctors found this to be a tough case.

The first thing I told this man was that, in the Christian faith, the soul, the personality that is 'me,' was given to him by God and that is the only thing that matters. Regarding his personal imperfections, like lack of confidence, shame, indecisiveness, and other issues, he should accept these things as they are. I advised him to take it easy, don't be resentful, and just accept who he is. In Christianity, God said that was enough. This is called God's Love. God looks at the intrinsic virtue in people; he is not concerned with their outward appearance. He just accepts them as they are.

Over the course of many discussions, his attitude changed and he started to face his personal challenges on his own. In fact, just coming to church was, in itself, a sign that he had already started down the road toward improvement. Being able to practice his faith is what made him think he had the power to change on his own. We discussed how he was given a personality that is 'me' and nothing but 'me' by God and that because he was given a new life through God he should respect himself first and then do his best to respect others around him. At the same time, I thought it was important to teach him that when he faced a dilemma that was difficult to resolve, he should ask God for help and leave it in his hands.

Also, I always tell people who are seeing doctors that there will be those they like and those who are not a good match, so they should find one that is a good fit. Eventually, this man was able to find one with whom he was comfortable.

How do other religions and philosophies view the concept of an imperfect 'me'? The following is an amusing anecdote:

> A high school administered a test in which students needed to score 70 points or more in order to pass. If they scored below that, they would not advance to the next grade. One of the students earned only 69 points.
>
> A teacher who was a member of the Communist Party would probably say to the student: "Shame on you for not working hard enough to pass, but since we have too many students who earned

perfect scores, we will take a point from one of them and give it to you. You passed."

A teacher who was a Buddhist monk might say: "What a pity! If you had only earned one more point you would have passed. But, as they say, 'That's life.' Accept it."

A Muslim teacher might say: "This is what you get for being lazy!"

A Christian teacher might say: "You missed by one point. Advance to the next class and work harder to make up for this shortcoming."

There may be Christian students who would be happy that their teachers let them get away with not meeting the standard, would rest on their laurels, or not work hard, but even that is okay. God is not concerned with such trivial affairs. Those who know they are truly loved and love themselves, though, would probably not behave that way.

The Student Who Confided, "For Me, There Is No *Today*"

I also happened to counsel a very young woman. She was a student of mine at Aoyama Gakuin, and we discussed an essay she wrote titled, "For Me, There is No *Today*." Slightly concerned and wondering if this was a philosophical treatise or if it reflected her actual circumstances, I asked her about it.

She explained: "For as long as I can remember, I have been going to school. At first it was, 'Go to school so you can get into a good kindergarten.' Then, when I entered kindergarten, it was, 'Go to school so you can get into a good elementary school.' Then, when I was in elementary school, it was, 'Go to cram school so you can get into a good middle school.' Even in middle school, it was, 'Go to cram school so you can get into a good high school,' and so on. No doubt, even after I get a job my parents will continue to insist, 'Get a good husband,' 'be a good wife,' and even 'raise good children.' My friends seem to be having fun, but I am not living for today but for tomorrow. What should I do about this?"

She was suffering from low self-esteem. Not once in her life had she disobeyed her parents. At the same time, I understood the sentiments of her parents who pushed her to work hard in school because they wanted her to have a good life in the future. However, this pressure put her under tremendous stress.

I first told her that I understood her dilemma. Then I advised: "You may consider this to be disrespectful to your parents, but you should think about taking a break from your studies now and then to pursue something you enjoy. Why don't you have a heart-to-heart talk with them about this?" She said she would when she returned home.

Advising people to do good deeds, not only so they can get into Heaven after they die but so they can also have a bright future here on Earth, and to continue with their spiritual training is, I feel, putting first things first. Don't all people, at some point in their lives, carry around some kind of emotional burden like this girl?

Among the parishioners of Komaba Eden Church, there are those who talk about their personal problems right away and those who only open up after a long time, but I can usually identify those who are in some sort of emotional distress when I see them. When someone is wracked with worry or deeply hurt by something they seem to have less energy. Also, the most difficult thing for a person to endure is having his or her character assailed. This amounts to nothing less than weakening or injuring the soul. Christianity teaches that we should strive to save our souls. At first glance, this, like the concept of original sin, is difficult to understand, but this is really the same as saving the personality that is 'me.'

As they continue going to church and are accepted there, their disposition gradually changes. They start to express themselves more openly and with greater confidence, and their outlook on life becomes more cheerful. Of course, this is due to the prayers and efforts of the individual, but I also think the fact that people make new friends at church is a big influence. This feels the same as when someone's fear in kendo goes away after they come to understand Ittō-ryū's kiriotoshi.

Is Monotheism the Origin of War?

People who are troubled are not the only ones who come to visit me. At times, I am forced to address the responsibility the Christian faith has as a monotheistic religion. What I am most often asked is if Christianity is the cause of wars because of its strong self-righteousness that comes from its exclusivity. Certainly, in a monotheistic religion, in which believers claim that their god is the best and all others are illegitimate, it is an undeniable fact that exclusivity exists. But I disagree with the premise that Christianity is the cause of wars,

The desire to fight is a part of human nature. When this desire to fight grows, people create a *casus belli*. As it is used as a pretext to assuage their own consciences, nothing beats religion as a convenient tool to mobilize the masses and recruit armies. Once the fighting starts, they then pray for divine protection. In other words, men co-opt Christianity to serve their own purposes.

I think there needs to be an effective way to defend religion against this kind of misuse, but in reality this would be very difficult. This is because there are two aspects to religion: the personal beliefs of the individual and the influence of the society in which they live. Once people become involved in war, the social dynamic becomes very strong. In the famous words of the American theologian Reinhold Niebuhr, "Evil is not to be traced back to the individual, but to the collective behavior of all humanity." This is how wars start. Once war begins, individuals lose the freedom to follow their own convictions.

Wars were often started in the past to spread religion. That was certainly true even for the first jihad of Islam, in which an Arab force fought the Sasanian Empire of Persia at the Battle of Nahavand in 642 shortly after the death of the prophet Muhammad, but wars of this type have all but disappeared today. Even the current Israeli-Palestinian conflict is about territorial expansion and their common history, not about forcing a religious conversion on the other. Furthermore, when looked at historically, especially in Asia, there have been wars between Buddhists and Muslims, mass slaughter by Pol Pot, and also conflicts between Hindus and Buddhists. It is fair to say that these horrific wars were not caused only by monotheistic religions.

As for those who make an issue of the exclusivity of Christianity, it seems that, in many cases, those making that charge believe Japanese people to be tolerant of all religions. This is because they respect the Japanese practice of paying homage to a countless number of gods. I have no intention to criticize this practice but would like others to take the opportunity to reconsider how they worship these deities.

The Convenience of the Power Spot Tour

In Japan, people believe in many gods, such as a god of water, a god that calms earthquakes, a god of business success, a god of fortune, a god of matchmaking, and even a god of the soil. Of course, such kinds of deities do not really exist, but people claim they receive miracles from them and then sell charms purported to bring good luck to their owners. Today, however, the reputations of these deities have grown and various shrines have become famous for being spiritually powerful, or having *power spots*–areas thought to be flowing with mystical energy–on their premises.

For example, a young student who is preparing to take an important test in school may decide to go to a shrine to pray to the god of academics and also drop by a shrine on the way home to pray to the god of matchmaking. The student may make such wishes as, "I want a high score on my examination," and "I want a boyfriend." In actuality, this student is asking the gods to make it very convenient for her to meet someone in school, during after-school studies, or on the way home.

When you think about it, this is not really a problem, but isn't there something strange about asking a deity for this kind of help? Would the student in this example really head straight to the shrine to thank the gods if she were to find a boyfriend? Is it really part of her faith that she asks for whatever she wants, whenever she likes? I cannot help but feel that, recently, television shows and magazines especially have emphasized stories regarding phenomena seemingly related to power spots.

In a polytheistic world view, people choose their own gods. From a Christian standpoint, this reflects a religious viewpoint in which one seeks to obtain material benefit in this world. Furthermore, believing that gods live in each tree and rock is not polytheism but pantheism. If people had not had such beliefs, they would have not placed such a high value on the natural resources required to live in this world, so this way of thinking was extremely wise.

Of course, polytheism is not limited to Japan. Even in the world of Greek mythology the gods played various roles in people's daily lives. As this kind of belief has developed in every corner of the globe, it reflects the sincere desire of all people to pursue a happier existence. They thought that the more they called on the gods to intervene, the more favors they would receive from them and the easier their lives would be.

There are also times I think the Japanese people do not see value in the absolute existence of God. Said another way, they trust their fellow human beings more than any god. There is a saying, "God is looking at you" (*tendosama*), but the word *god* has perhaps a more secular meaning, referring to such things as neighbors and the world in general rather than a supreme being. I cannot help but feel that this is a world view centered on Man.

In 2011, after the Great Eastern Japan Earthquake, a middle school student came to visit.

"When I was watching TV," she said, "I saw Christians praying for the Japanese victims. I was surprised to learn that they pray for other people. Can you teach me these Christian prayers?"

Up to that point, this young woman seemed to think that a prayer was merely asking for what she wanted for herself. Of course, in Christianity there are times when you tell God what you want but only after first offering up your daily thanks and then praying for the happiness of your neighbors. Making a prayer is not the same as asking for a miracle.

More specifically, prayers are not meditation or achieving spiritual enlightenment but the act of calling to God and receiving an answer from him. This is a difficult concept to grasp because it is not like hearing a response from another human being but is a dialogue between a person and God. The response from God can be likened to when you stare at a painting and it calls out to you, saying, "something is here," even though you don't hear a voice. In the Bible, even dreams can be considered a type of revelation which contains answers to requests from this world.

Today, when even in Europe and the Americas the number of dedicated Christians is dwindling, spreading the Word of God within Japan is considered a daunting task. Whether it was during the Great East Japan Earthquake, during debates in the Diet, or even during a recent high-school bullying scandal in Otsu City, Shiga Prefecture,[44] I was worried when I saw that adults were running around in total confusion. In the past, they would

---

[44] In October 2011, after being repeatedly bullied by his classmates at his middle school in Otsu City, Shiga Prefecture, a thirteen year old boy killed himself. This case garnered national and international attention after it came to light that school officials not only knew of the bullying and failed to stop it but also attempted to cover up the fact that the suicide was the direct result of this bullying. Trans.

have talked from a position of moral authority but that opportunity has been lost. Our sense of values has become so watered down that we are losing the ability to explain among adults, and even to children, why something is good, why it is bad, and what should be respected.

There is no sense of absolute right and wrong within society anymore. An illustration of this is when one of the teenagers responsible for bullying a fellow student in Otsu City mockingly commented in a television interview, "We were just having fun." This may sound like I am interpreting the facts to fit my argument, but without faith, people truly do not know what is right and what is wrong.

Even Akutagawa Ryunosuke wrote about this in his book, *Seiho no hito*. He opined that doing good deeds comes from a sense of morality. This sense of morality comes from the conscience. What is considered conscientious changes over time; however, if God is absolute, then the small voice in your head that tells you what is right or wrong remains unshakeable.

In the philosophical sense, the term *values* encompasses truth, goodness and beauty. The pursuit of truth is reason, and, academically, philosophy. Pursuit of virtue is understanding, and, academically, logic. Pursuit of aesthetics is sensory contemplation, and, academically, the arts. The sense of what is considered righteous and beautiful will transform over time.

Also, when it comes to love, there is the corruptible kind of love and mistaken love. Variety is okay, but I would like to see people reach for and thoroughly examine absolute love.

When asked what the most important thing in life was, Jesus answered: "You shall love the Lord your God with all your heart, and with all your soul, and with all your mind. The second is this, 'You shall love your neighbor as yourself.' By doing so, you will know the true nature of love. There is no other commandment greater than these." His words do not mean you should search out a neighbor you should love, but to make a neighbor of a person who is in need.

In my view, the basic idea behind the concepts of 'holy' or 'sacred' that are described in religion is nothing more than making this sense of values absolute. If something is sacred, it is uncorrupted and pure. When this idea is expressed in the Japanese language, it comes very close to the concepts of honor and love. I believe that Japanese people, who already understand both honor and love through Bushido, would be ahead of the game if they were to put Christianity to practical use. If they had just been able to learn the lessons of the Bible earlier in history, Christianity would have taken root in Japan more so than in any other country.

Carrying on the Traditions of the Church That Doubles as a Dojo

When a massive hurricane struck the American city of New Orleans in 2005, there was a tremendous amount of looting in the neighborhoods hit by the disaster. When Japanese citizens were placed in a similar situation during the Great East Japan Earthquake, the victims of the disaster earned the respect of the world through the calm and orderly manner in which they responded.

It has been about a thousand years from when the samurai first appeared during the Heian era. Bushido, which has continued to develop since then, seems to be gradually fading into the past, but I believe that it has completely permeated the DNA of the Japanese people. I would like to think it possible that, when push comes to shove, the spirit of Bushido will be manifest in their actions. In today's Japan, though they may not be conspicuous, there are certainly people who try to live their lives according to the code of Bushido, and so I don't believe that Bushido has completely disappeared.

For decades I have been invited to the foreign nations of Republic of San Marino, Italy, Germany, United States, Turkey, and others where I delivered lectures and taught classes related to both Christianity and Ittō-ryū. Westerners believe that the calm, post-war recovery of Japan and the politeness and orderliness of Japanese society come from Bushido. It seems that foreigners, more so than the Japanese, enthusiastically embrace its spirit.

I also often hear from people in those countries that we should merge the faith of Christianity with Bushido, the traditional spirit of Japan, to create a new and peaceful world. It is my sense that they anticipate that the result would not be Western-style Christianity, but a new style of Christianity that is born from Bushido and which brings out the best characteristics of East and West. In other words, they long for the ideal of both Christianity, with its strong sense of morals, and the lofty ethics that come from the spirit of Bushido.

Martial arts became a compulsory subject of physical education in Japanese middle schools starting in April of 2012. My undying wish is to see an increase in the number of those young people who develop an interest in Bushido after having an opportunity to learn martial arts.

But, as I have written many times before, it is difficult for Christianity to quickly spread within Japan. However, I believe that fostering a Christian spirit within Japan will certainly become more and more necessary in the years ahead. The number of suicides in Japan has topped thirty-thousand a year. When you include the numbers of those who suffer from depression and who are mentally ill, this number could double or even go much higher. As I wrote at the beginning of this chapter, I think there are many among those who are suffering who could be helped by embracing Christianity. A person's thinking and outlook on life greatly changes after accepting the existence of God. When their outlook changes, their personal relations with those around them improve and they also become more emotionally stable. There are other examples of this in my church too.

The avant-garde artist Kusama Yayoi has been a friend of mine since I worked in a church in New York City. I was able to get to know her when she lived there and visited our church to talk or share her feelings. She did not come to worship, but we ministers who worked there became her friends and thought we had been able to ease her mind a bit. As can be seen in her autobiography, *Mugen no ami – Kusama yayoi jiden*, she was able to produce many artistic works at this time in her life.

As we face a future in which society is rapidly aging, we are likely to see an increase in the number of people who live alone. The church will be able to provide a sense of community for them. Belonging to a church is not just about having friends but can also ease the fear of death. It can also lessen the burden on families who struggle with how to keep up with the various memorial services and ceremonies that are traditionally done in Japan.

As I have a wonderful opportunity to continue studying both Christianity and Ittō-ryū, I would like for both of these Ways to continue to flourish within Japan. Though the prospects for both may be somewhat modest, I still think I should continue to calmly and patiently talk about their merits. Whether the martial arts or Christianity, if I continue to preserve the true meaning of both of these Ways, other people are bound to be attracted by them and follow these same paths. I consider it my life's mission to continue to pass on the lesson of these Ways in my work at the Komaba Eden Church.

Afterword

I feel a renewed sense of gratitude to those who come to me, a minister and successor of a traditional martial arts school, to seek advice. This is because I gain insight into how they view both Bushido and Christianity and also refine my own understanding while answering their questions.

After engaging in these discussions, though, I am concerned that although the people of Japan have some superficial knowledge of Christianity, they don't have a deep understanding of what it is really about. For one thing, I have no doubt that they would say that Christianity is something imported from the West. Christianity certainly spread to what is now the Western world at an early time in history. Because Westerners were the driving force behind it in the modern world and also played a major role as evangelists in Japan, Japanese tend not to realize that it first came from the Middle East. It even spread to Asia, India, and China.

In Japan's past, the spirit of absorbing education and cultural development from foreign countries used to be very strong, as can be seen in the old slogans: "Japanese Spirit Imbued with Chinese Learning," and "Japanese Spirit Imbued with Western Learning," and I sense that this trend has continued into the present. You could also say that one drawback to this is that the Japanese people believe the good thing in these equations is Japan's soul, or *tamashii* (魂), but neither accept its foreign analog nor try to really understand it.

Christianity is not merely an intellectual or educational pursuit but a spiritual Way that closely examines life and death. Its fundamental purpose has never been merely to serve the West, but all of mankind. If they were to understand this foundation, I believe the Japanese people would certainly be able to accept this faith.

At the same time, I don't think the Christian world, even including those Japanese who are Christians, have ever fully understood Japan or the psychology of the East and the teachings of Bushido. When I translated Original Sin from English to Japanese, I wrote that it is close to the meaning of the word *karma*, but feel I need to study the nuances of Japan more closely, to include how words like this should be more accurately interpreted.

I would be eternally grateful if this book were to begin to bridge the gap between the Japanese and Christian ways of thinking. As I have described many times, Christianity is a sacred and dignified faith that is sought throughout the world. If they were to put aside preconceived ideas about it and be open to it, I believe Japanese people in particular would become good Christians. Furthermore, if the spirit of Japanese Bushido and Christianity–not just the Christianity which is exclusive to Europe and the Americas but Christianity with Japanese characteristics–were to spread throughout the world, peace, justice and tranquility would prevail.

In closing, if it were not for the guidance of my late father and mother, I would never have had the conviction to bring the two Ways of Christianity and Bushido together. Being raised by my father, who was a Christian, a martial arts master, and an educator, and my mother, who shared my father's faith and was a teacher of both the Japanese language and history, it was only natural that I would embrace both Ways from a young age.

    The dream of my parents, especially in their twilight years, was to devote everything they had, including their home, to the Church and dojo. Today, I am greatly assisted in every aspect of my work at the Komaba Eden Church that they established by my wife, who also shares my faith. In the future, I may continue to experience hardships and suffering, but the Ways that I should follow are laid out before me.

    I would like to express my deepest gratitude to: Uchida Misaho, who provided the opportunity to introduce this book to the world; members of the Komaba Eden Church and my students of Ittō-ryū; Miyazawa Yasuyuki, who assisted with photography; and also both Kado Fumiko and Yoshizawa Hiroki of Shinchosha Inc. for their tremendous assistance.

Works Cited

Akutagawa Ryunosuke. *Seiho no hito*. First published in 1927.

Clark, William. Prepared for the students of the Sapporo Agricultural College. "Covenant of Believers in Jesus." Sapporo: 1877.

Confucius. *The Spring and Autumn Annals (Shunju Sashiden)*. N.p. [thought to have been written 722-481 BCE and edited by Confucius some time later.]

Kiyomizu Kiyoshi. *Ankoku nikki* (暗黒日記 1942-1945). Tokyo: Iwanami Bunko, 2004

Nakazato Kaizan. *Daibosatsu toge*. Tokyo: 1981.

Nelson, Andrew N. *The Modern Reader's Japanese-English Character Dictionary*, 2nd revised edition. Tokyo: Charles E. Tuttle Co. Inc., 1962.

Nitobe, Inazo. *Bushido: the Soul of Japan*. N.p. 1899. Reprinted by Ohara Publications, 1979.

Oeno Masafusa. *Tōsenkyō* (闘戦経). N.p., [thought to have been written circa 1100]

Uchimura, Kanzo. *How I became a Christian: Out of My Diary*. Tokyo: Iwanami Bunko, first published in 1895.

Uchimura Kanzo. *Representative Men of Japan: Essays,* Tokyo: 1908

Uchimura Kanzo, *Shinko chosaku zenshu*, Tokyo: Iwanami Shoten, 1933, Volume 23

Watase Tsuneyoshi. *Ebina Danjo sensei*, N.p, n.d.

Yamamoto Tsunetomo. *Hagakure, the Secret Wisdom of the Samurai*. Translated by Alexander Bennett. Tokyo: Tuttle Publishing, 2014

Appendix: Ono-ha Ittō-ryū Lineage Chart (abbreviated)

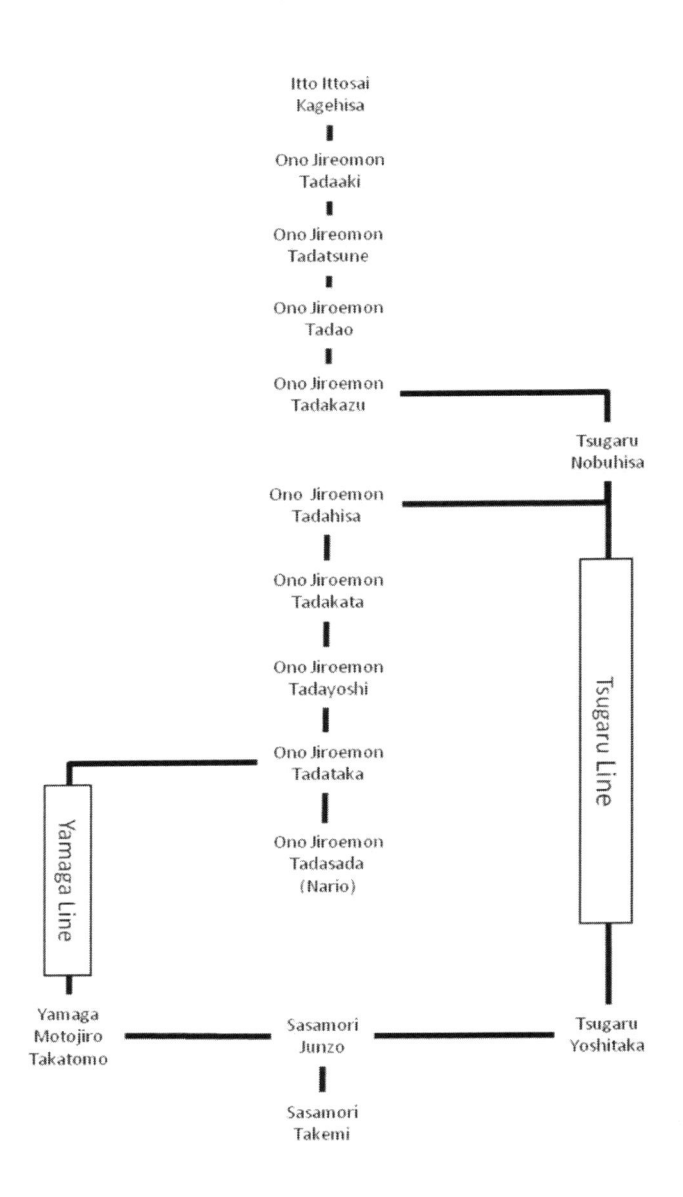

Itto Ittosai Kagehisa
↓
Ono Jireomon Tadaaki
↓
Ono Jireomon Tadatsune
↓
Ono Jiroemon Tadao
↓
Ono Jiroemon Tadakazu ——————————→ Tsugaru Nobuhisa
↓
Ono Jiroemon Tadahisa ———————————|
↓
Ono Jiroemon Tadakata
↓
Ono Jiroemon Tadayoshi
↓
Ono Jiroemon Tadataka
↓
Ono Jiroemon Tadasada (Nario)

Yamaga Line | Tsugaru Line

Yamaga Motojiro Takatomo —— Sasamori Junzo —— Tsugaru Yoshitaka
↓
Sasamori Takemi

About the Author

Born in Hirosaki City, Japan, as the third and youngest son of martial arts legend Sasamori Junzo, the Reverend Sasamori Takemi was raised in a household where the ethics of the samurai, martial arts, and Christianity were part of daily life. After graduating from Waseda and Aoyama Gakuin Universities with Bachelor of Arts degrees in Sociology and Theology, he continued his studies in the United States where he attended the Duke University School of Divinity and the Hartford Seminary Foundation, earning Masters of Arts Degrees in Christian and Religious Education. He also served as both Assistant and Associate Minister at the United Church of Christ in New York City for nine years. Upon returning to Japan in 1969, he became the founding minister of the Komaba Eden Church, Setagaya Ward, Tokyo, where, assisted by his wife Ariko, he ministers to over one hundred fifty parishioners. In 1975, he was officially recognized as the 17th Sōke of Ono-ha Ittō-ryū, as well as the Sōke of the Shinmusō Hayashizaki-ryū school of iaido and the Chokugen-ryū school of naginata. He has over five hundred martial arts students world-wide and instructs annually in Japan, Asia, Europe and the United States. Regularly featured in the Japanese media, he has published or been featured in nine publications and four videos on both Christianity and the martial arts. He served on the Board of Trustees of the Japanese Traditional Martial Arts Association for over 35 years and was awarded a Doctor of Divinity from the California Graduate School of Theology in 1989.

About the Translator

Mark Hague retired from the U.S. Army at the rank of colonel after thirty years of active military service, twenty-five years of which were in overseas posts. After serving in operational assignments as an infantry officer with the 25th Infantry Division (Light) in Hawaii and the 6th Infantry Division (Light) in Alaska, he became a Foreign Area Officer in 1996 and subsequently served over eighteen years in various assignments in Japan and Hawaii. His last position was the Director, Strategic Plans and Policy J5 of Headquarters, United States Forces, Japan where he focused on strategic planning, policy implementation, interagency coordination, and realigning U.S. military bases within Japan. A life-long martial artist, he has practiced various types of martial arts since he was sixteen years old and has achieved dan rankings in several styles. He started training in Ono-ha Ittō-ryū under Sasamori Sōke in 2002 and was awarded the Kanajisho Mokuroku in 2009. He continues to train in the Reigakudo dojo in Tokyo.

Printed in Great Britain
by Amazon